John —

"TUPANDE KILELENI"

"Let's Cling to the Summit, Together!"

Hope you enjoy the stories of this journey to & within Tanzania, which impacted every traveler.

Kileleni!

[signature]

November 2022

"Let China sleep for if she wakes..."
Napoleon

1994 has been a Landmark
year for China. 70 years
of living dangerously.
Making, losing trillions
in the last 30.

TUPANDE KILELENI

Let's Climb to the Summit Together

Patrick Steenberge

Create your team; develop their dream.

Copyright © 2018 by Patrick Steenberge.

Library of Congress Control Number: 2017911803
ISBN: Hardcover   978-1-5434-4056-0
              Softcover   978-1-5434-4055-3
              eBook   978-1-5434-4054-6

All rights reserved. No part of this book may be reproduced or transmitted in any form or by any means, electronic or mechanical, including photocopying, recording, or by any information storage and retrieval system, without permission in writing from the copyright owner.

Any people depicted in stock imagery provided by Getty Images are models, and such images are being used for illustrative purposes only.
Certain stock imagery © Getty Images.

Print information available on the last page.

Rev. date: 02/13/2018

To order additional copies of this book, contact:
Xlibris
1-888-795-4274
www.Xlibris.com
Orders@Xlibris.com
764461

Contents

Foreword for Tupande Kileleni xi

Introduction: "It's Kili Time! Make the Most of It." xxiii

1 One Man's Dream—the Commitment of Many 1
2 Mexico Joins the Team 17
3 In God's Hands from the Beginning 29
4 Exploring Tanzania—the Albino Baboon 37
5 It's Not the X's and O's, It's the Jims and Joes 67
6 We Have No Breaking Point!
   (Ara's most memorable quote) 85
7 Adjust with Poise 101
8 JR + Muhammad + Andre = Game Stadium 109
9 If It Were Easy, Everyone Would Do It 135
10 Love Grows When People Serve 151
11 Safari—Lions, Leopards, And Ticks…Oh My! 163
12 *Tupande Kileleni*—
   Let's Climb to the Summit Together! 175
13 Climbing Realities—Life Lessons—Mil Gracias 199

This book, the account of incredible teamwork across
nations and continents, as well as commitment among so many
caring people, has made it to print through
the amazing efforts of Caitlin Zematis, my niece,
daughter of my dear sister, Colleen.
This simply would not have happened without her!
Asante Sana!

As this book is an account of many people's efforts, taking one man's dream to heart and having no breaking point in our multinational effort to achieve a stated goal, so it has been in getting this story into print. Every person mentioned in the following pages played an instrumental role in creating and living this story, in making it so special for everyone involved. As you read about the broad range of challenges and accomplishments that helped forge the Global Kilimanjaro Bowl into a story that I hope will inspire and motivate you, you will realize that the project would have remained simply personal memories of the participants if not for those who took the next step.

From the moment I returned from Tanzania in June 2011, I was constantly told by friends and family, "You need to write a book!"

Now that this is completed, I realize just what a team effort it has been to gather all the pertinent details and stories and memories, put them together into a coherent, compelling story, attempting to capture the true spirit of the individuals who believed in the mantra, *Tupande Kileleni* (Let's climb to the summit together).

As with the entire project, the leaders for this book were the dreamers/doers spanning three distinct cultures and lands. In America's heartland, Coach Chris Creighton and Drake University Director of Athletics Sandy Hatfield Clubb provided unending faith, belief, and trust.

In Mexico, Dr. Enrique Ramos of Tec de Monterrey University would simply inquire periodically, "How is the book coming? You really need to tell this story." In his gently persuasive manner, he would remind me just how important this account could be for those who were part of it, and for others needing inspiration in their lives.

From Tanzania, Africa, I could always count on Frank Mella, managing director of Kilele Savane, Ltd. to help me recreate many of the scenes as they actually took place, identifying the people involved and how the heck we got through some of the more tenuous moments on tour. He coined the title to this book long ago, although he didn't realize it at the time.

The continued ascent of Lazaro Nyalandu to his current position as Minister of Natural Resources and Tourism drives me to further assist Tanzania through the development and promotion of sports, ecotourism, and experiential education. His success and support also motivate me to help fund, through the revenue from this publication, more and more fresh water wells for the people of his native Singida Region.

Then there are the "worker/believers" who would not allow me to forget my goal of actually telling this story in print so all can recall, when we are older and a bit slower of mind and foot: Caitlin Zematis (writer), Colleen Zematis (editor), Mel Greenberg (editor), Mike Preston (publicist), Don Weller (cover art), Georgia Steenberge (cover graphic design), Janet (my wife and quiet strength), Georgia and Brier and Xela—our simply amazing children who so embrace the world and all its wonders.

To view a four-minute highlight video of all the action in Tanzania, search YouTube for "Tupande Kileleni

Tupande Kileleni!

Foreword for Tupande Kileleni

The two weeks in May of 2011 that those of us from the Drake Football program, the Mexican CONADEIP All-Star, the Global Football team, and our many gracious hosts in Tanzania got to experience together were truly incredible. When I reflect back on the entirety of this experience, the trip itself was the culmination of a two-year long journey shared by a special group of people who believed that the vision of taking a football team to Africa to play a game, serve and experience the local community, and climb Mt. Kilimanjaro could become a reality and that providing this opportunity would be worth the effort, energy, and time required to try to make it happen.

Despite our determined efforts, it became clear at the outset and throughout the process that this vision was not going to come together easily. In fact, at various times along the way we would come up against an obstacle that we simply could not overcome. It was at these moments and in these situations that God in His time and in His own way would open the door and allow us to pursue the next step. It was as if He was saying—this is going to happen and yes it is going to be beyond what you had envisioned but it is a gift from me and not a result of anything else. How this trip came together was as significant as the actual trip itself.

This entire experience will forever be one of the most incredible of my life. Asante Sana, Sandy Hatfield Clubb, for saying, "let's make it happen," in the late summer of 2009.

Asante Sana, Enrique Ramos, for committing the Mexican contingent to this crazy idea three days before our trip cancellation deadline in July 2010. Asante Sana to all the players, coaches, staff, family and friends from three different countries who participated in this adventure and for making this such a meaningful and unforgettable experience for so many.

Finally, Asante Sana to Patrick Steenberge for saying "Yes!" to the out of the blue question, "Do you want to do something big, really big?" back in January of 2010, and now for taking the time and effort to put down on paper so many wonderful memories for all of us to remember and relive. And for others to read, to dream and to reach out to others who will help them succeed in a huge way.

—Coach Chris Creighton
Drake University
Head Coach

Tupande Kileleni!

There are experiences in life that leave an indelible imprint on your soul. Serving as a member of the team that created the Global Kilimanjaro Bowl, and the journey that accompanied it, is one of those experiences for me.

Three countries, two universities, and hundreds of people came together to share in a two-week trip involving community service, a trek up the highest free standing mountain in the world, and a collegiate football game. The extraordinary experience was a result of a collaborative effort birthed from a coach's dream to lead his team up Mount Kilimanjaro in Tanzania, Africa.

It could only happen by grace that Drake University found an opponent that would travel around the world to play football and engage its student-athletes in this atypical learning experience. Even after finding an opponent, the logistics seemed almost insurmountable—medical support was needed should a serious injury occur during the game; transportation, housing and a 6-day trek for 200 people needed coordination; a playable football field was needed in a country that has never seen American style football; and more. It was the belief and actions of a number of people that created history through an extraordinary shared vision.

Head Drake Football Coach, Chris Creighton had a dream; Global Football Founder and President, Patrick Steenberge had the foresight and outstanding coordination efforts; Tecnológico de Monterrey's National Director of Student Affairs, Dr. Enrique Ramos shared a vision for extraordinary student learning experiences; Kilele Savane, Ltd. owner, Frank Mella, shared his unbelievable organizational capability and Tanzanian relationships; Del Christensen and his Iowa Resource for International Service flawlessly coordinated all community service; Orthopedic Surgeon Dr. Steve Meyer coordinated medical efforts; and I received a blessing of a lifetime helping to connect the dots.

—Sandy Hatfield Clubb
Drake University
Director of Athletics

Foreword

I was so thrilled to be involved in the May 2011 Kili Bowl Event, the dream of the American Football coach that came true. Many people from USA, Mexico and Tanzania were involved in that historical event that had never happened on the African continent before, and I am so grateful to have been a part of it as the ground operator! Tupande Kileleni.

It was not an easy task to implement and accomplish the whole program, but through the power of God all obstacles were overcome and things went smoothly throughout. There was hard work and encouragement from many good willing people who took this dream seriously and kept working on it until it became true!

The event had both economical and social benefits to many Tanzanians. I believe that everyone in Tanzania who participated in this event has learned a great deal about the cultures from United States and Mexico. The sport was previously completely unknown to many Tanzanians, and we have learned that the American football game has much to do with solidarity. Through that event, we were able to bring together many local schools' students to meet, to learn, to play and to share experiences with Americans and Mexicans. The visiting student athletes enjoyed sharing their time, giving their time to build and paint school buildings and orphanage centers in the Moshi/Kilimanjaro region. Economically there were many businessmen that benefited from the event by offering various services such as tours, accommodations, transportations, food, souvenirs etc. There were also a large number of people who were hired to work for the two weeks of the event.

One of the most impressive parts of the event that I will always remember after the football game is the Mount Kilimanjaro climb, whereas there were 77 climbers from USA and 58 from Mexico. 75 out 77 from USA made it to the top and 45 out of 58 from Mexico made it to the top which makes the total number of 121 people from one group who stood on the roof of Africa at a time. There was no such history on Kili before! I hope that this event will be recognized all over the world and that all who participated will remain to be good willing ambassadors of our beautiful country Tanzania, the Land of Mount Kilimanjaro.

I wish to express my sincere thanks to Sandra Clubb, the Drake Athletic Director for highly recommending my company and introducing me to Patrick Steenberge. Thank you Patrick, the president of Global Football for accepting my company and cooperating with me until the end of the event. I would also like to thank all the official staff from Drake University and CONADEIP, including the coaches, students and fans. Finally, I would like to thank all the Tanzanian government officials, especially from the Ministry of Sports and Culture, and the Ministry of Tourism for their effort to facilitate the Kili Bowl event and assuring good security to everybody.

Frank Mella
Managing Director
Kilele Savane Ltd.

Tupande Kileleni!

In my role as the Tec de Monterrey Director of Student Affairs, my professional goals are to promote and foster student growth and personal development, guided by a holistic approach to learning which are congruent with the institution's academic mission. While I have participated in many programs, activities, projects and so forth during my career, I have never participated in anything that has accomplished the aforementioned goals in such a way as the Global Kilimanjaro Bowl.

There are a myriad of stories and anecdotes that all of us who participated in this life changing experience share. Beyond that however, the 'Kili Bowl' has also brought about personal, and professional reflections that without a doubt have contributed to making us better persons who acknowledge how fortunate we were to have taken part in this incredible journey.

I want to thank everybody that made this dream possible, especially Coach Creighton, Sandy Clubb, Patrick Steenberge, and Dr. Carlos Mijares, who believed in and supported this mission. Many lives are much better because of your commitment, courage, and direction, but mainly because of the love you have for your students. We all shared a common dream and we each did our part to make it possible; job well done.

May God bless us in such a way that our paths cross again somewhere along the road.

Dr. Enrique Ramos
Tec de Monterrey University
Director of Student Affairs

Tupande Kileleni!

(As printed in the Global Kilimanjaro Bowl Game Program)

In the past decade I have had the chance to travel with Coach Chris Creighton as he led his teams to Austria and Panama. We are kindred spirits in travel, adventure and our belief that we who are so fortunate should reach out, lead, experience, learn from cultures, and help others as possible.

Life changed in January 2010 when Coach told me of his dream, supported by Drake athletic director, Sandy Hatfield Clubb, and asked me to find an opponent that would share this dream and travel to Africa to play. Seven months later, Student Affairs Director Enrique Ramos of Tec de Monterrey University Mexico, heartily embraced the same vision, believing strongly that students should become global citizens. So CONADEIP became our true partners; a blessing indeed!

Now we work together, preparing to do something very special and historical, something that will impact the lives of the college student athletes from Mexico and the US who travel to Tanzania to compete, to live out an adventure, and to serve. They will in turn impact the lives of thousands of youngsters in Tanzania, now and in the future. In addition, we will bring a dynamic team sport to Africa, known as American football.

We have a stellar 'team' working to achieve all our goals, and many newfound friends in Tanzania have joined in the effort. Thanks to the introduction of Iowan Dr. Steve Meyer, Deputy Minister Lazaro Nyalandu has been key to leading us to the right leaders in his nation. Frank Mella and his Kilele Savane group will take care of our transport, safari and Kilimanjaro climb; while TANAPA (Tanzania National Parks Association) and TAHA, (Tanzania Horticulture Association) are instrumental in their support, as well as dozens of others.

So I say to you the most common word in Swahili, 'Karibu', or Welcome. Please join us as we strive to always climb to the summit, "Tupande Kileleni".

Asante Sana (thank you),
Patrick Steenberge
President, Global Football

Tupande Kileleni!

En los últimos diez años he tenido la oportunidad de viajar a Austria y Panamá con el entrenador en jefe de la Universidad de Drake, Chris Creighton y su equipo de fútbol americano. El entrenador Creighton y yo somos como almas gemelas. Creemos que las personas que son tan afortunados como nosotros debemos aprender de otras culturas, proveer un modelo de liderazgo y ayudar a los demás tan a menudo como sea posible.

La vida cambió en enero de 2010 cuando el entrenador Creighton me habló de su sueño para llevar a cabo el Tazón Global Kilimanjaro. Con el apoyo de la Directora de Deportes de Drake Sandy Hatfield Clubb, él me pidió que encontrara a un oponente que compartiera este sueño. Siete meses más tarde en México, el Director de Asuntos Estudiantiles del Sistema Tecnológico de Monterrey el Dr. Enrique Ramos respaldó con beneplácito la visión de celebrar un juego en África. Así, la CONADEIP se convirtió en nuestra socia - una verdadera bendición en verdad!

Ahora, estamos trabajando juntos para preparar una experiencia muy especial que cambiará la vida de los estudiantes-atletas de México y los EE.UU. Ellos vivirán una aventura y en el proceso, ayudarán a miles de jóvenes en Tanzania. Además, vamos a traer un dinámico deporte de conjunto, conocido como el fútbol americano, a África.

Contamos con un equipo estelar de trabajo para lograr nuestros objetivos, entre ellos muchos nuevos amigos en Tanzania. El Viceministro Nyalandu Lázaro, que nos fue presentado por el Dr. Steve Meyer de Iowa, y que ha facilitado las conexiones con los líderes en su nación. El grupo Kilele Savane de Frank Mella, quien se encargará de nuestro transporte, safari y escalada al Kilimanjaro. La TANAPA (Asociación de Parques Nacionales de Tanzania) y la TAHA (Asociación de Horticultura de Tanzania) que juegan un papel decisivo con su apoyo, así como también docenas de otras organizaciones.

Así, os digo la palabra más común en Swahili, "Karibu", o "Bienvenido". Por favor, únanse a nosotros en nuestra lucha por siempre subir a la cumbre, "Tupande Kileleni".

Gracias,
Patrick Steenberge
Presidente de Global Football

Introduction

"It's Kili Time! Make the Most of It."

A dream kept to oneself remains a dream, but once shared with the right person, it can become reality.

> **Saturday, May 21, 2011, *ARUSHA, Tanzania*—**American football crossed a new international border on Saturday when the Drake University Bulldogs and the CONADEIP All-Stars from Mexico met on the gridiron, painted for the first time on African soil in Arusha, Tanzania.
>
> —GoDrakeBulldogs.com,
> Drake Athletics, Saturday May 21, 2011

With a 17-7 fourth-quarter comeback victory, Drake University won the Global Kilimanjaro Bowl, presented by TANAPA, in front of 11,781 curious but enthusiastic Tanzanian spectators at the Sheik Amri Abedi Memorial Stadium. Notably, this is where the Tanzanian flag was first raised in 1961, signaling its independence from Great Britain.

For the previous eighteen months, I had been working toward this dream, where Drake University and the CONADEIP Mexico League All-Stars would meet on Tanzanian soil in the first American football game on the African continent, sharing this historic moment in sports. The football game, however, was only one element of the overall journey. Like many dreams, this one wasn't solely my own and didn't come to me in my sleep. In fact, it didn't even originate with me! But in the end this wondrous dream was shared with hundreds, even thousands, of individuals who worked together as a team to make an improbable experience possible.

So how did this groundbreaking game, this first-of-its-kind event, this dream, come about?

I am a passionate traveler and explorer first, and a football guy second. Seems I have been this way since I was a child playing football with my three brothers in our corner yard on Arlington Road, while my father traveled to exotic places as a General Electric Finance Manager. In high school I was the starting quarterback at Cathedral Prep High School in Erie, Pennsylvania, coached by ex-ND lineman Tony Zambroski. I was then fortunate enough to play at the University of Notre Dame under legendary coach Ara Parseghian, who not only led Notre Dame in winning two national championships, but also was my coach when Notre Dame played in the Cotton Bowl, defeating the Texas Longhorns in 1971. For most athletes who do not go on to play pro ball, their sports careers come to a sudden halt after graduating from college, or they become coaches. Mine came to an untimely end, due to injury.

For a few years, I pursued other career interests involving travel, sports, marketing, media, and communications. I even worked for a while with troubled youth, outdoors in the wilderness. At the age of twenty-six, I embarked on a yearlong Latin America backpack adventure, visiting my folks in Brazil, where they were living at the time, which really expanded the wandering fever that I still maintain today. Through all my career twists and turns, football remained a keen interest, with travel as my passion.

In 1996, I started my own business venture, called Global Football. Since then I have been blessed to take amateur American football players, coaches and followers around the world to compete in international events, to learn firsthand about other cultures and to share their experiences with teammates. Amazingly, starting with Mt. St. Joseph High School and Coach Mike Working of Maryland to London on our first football tour, I have had the opportunity to organize tours for over 180 teams to travel to some twenty-one nations on six continents.

Saying that, I had never imagined creating a football event in Africa, a continent deeply rooted in tradition, and a mystery to many Americans, where the game we simply call "football" is completely foreign to the vast majority of the population. The dream came to me through a man for whom I already had great respect, Coach Chris Creighton of Drake University. Today, that respect has grown immensely due to his sharing this very special dream with me and then working together hand in hand over the next eighteen months to make his dream come true.

In January 2010, I attended the annual American Football Coaches (AFCA) Convention in Orlando. Every year the AFCA convention draws about ten thousand primarily large, engaging men who coach football for a living. I would say 80 percent of them are college coaches, the other 20 percent being a smattering of high school coaches and internationals, including some two hundred vendors like myself who use this occasion as an opportunity to speak directly with coaches. This is the one place every year where coaches and vendors get a chance to come together to share ideas, skills, products and services. I have rented a booth space there every year since 1997. From a business standpoint, it is the best place for me to meet with as many coaches as possible in a single location.

So there I was, standing in front of my fairly simple booth on a Monday morning, the second day of the event, chatting with coaches and old friends who walked by, discussing foreign travel, telling stories, shaking hands... when all of a sudden I was grabbed from behind, as coaches often do, by these two strong hands. I spun around and found myself looking eye to eye with Coach Chris Creighton of Drake University, who is fortunately about my size. He kind of slapped me upside the shoulder, and I did the same, then we gave each other a big bear hug.

We had grown close and become friends when he was a coach at Wabash College. He and I worked together to take his NCAA Division III teams first to Germany and Austria, and later to Panama before he took the job at Drake University. The first journey was memorable; the second was amazing!

After Coach Creighton and I were finished accosting each other, he just looked at me, and in his typically direct manner said,

"Hey, I've got a really big idea, I mean this one is big, are you in?"

I looked at him directly, paused just for a moment and without even questioning replied, "Sure…sure, I'm in."

When a guy I like and trust as much as Chris Creighton says he's got something big and asks if I am in, I immediately say yes! Only later do I ask what it is that I had just committed my life to. This attitude may stem back to a metal plaque I had hanging in my bedroom as a teenager, one of two. This one read, "Think before you act, but don't think too long; if you're not quick to react the chance will be gone."

The second plaque provided further motivation, "If you aren't a little bit scared, you ain't going fast enough."

Coach Creighton explained, "I want to take my Drake football team to climb Mt. Kilimanjaro and play the first American Football game ever in Africa. I have checked it out. There has never been a college or high school football game on the continent, only a few military ones. We could be the first to play football in Africa, and even more importantly, have our team provide community service projects to needy people there, and it would be the ultimate team building project to climb Mt. Kilimanjaro."

Creighton went on to explain how he had long held this dream of taking his football team to the summit of Mt. Kilimanjaro, Africa's tallest peak, and the world's largest free-standing mountain.

I asked, "Just how high is Kilimanjaro?"

"It's over nineteen thousand feet, just a bit over."

I'd climbed mountain summits in Colorado, Arizona, and New Mexico, some over fourteen thousand feet, as well as some passes over fifteen thousand feet in Peru and Bolivia long ago, so I knew it would be challenging but doable for a team of athletes.

So I went on to ask quite simply, "What do you want me to do?"

He clearly told me, "Everything. I have my team and will get them fired up to travel, and my Athletic Director is pumped about it. She climbed Kili years ago with her father. Our President is on board, and will likely go with us. So I just need *you* to do everything else. Find an opponent for us to play, find a stadium to play in, plan the logistics of the tour, figure out how to incorporate football, community service, a safari, and get us to the summit of Kili."

I sort of laughed and said, "Okay, I've got it."
So the journey began.

View from the Summit

None of this would have happened if I had deliberated over Coach Creighton's idea, analyzed it, figured out budgets and time needed to accomplish the dream, looked at dangers, profit and loss, etc. Call me crazy, but I am not that kind of person. I usually take an idea—especially one brought to me by a respected friend—a challenging and exciting one, and run with it. Most times it works, sometimes not, but why not give it a try? I had created and produced so many different football events over the years in such a variety of countries that I had a pretty good idea what an event like this would entail. Or so I thought. Now in retrospect I know I underestimated this challenge a bit, but it was well worth it!

I also imagined what it could mean to the football teams' members involved, the Tanzanians we would come in contact with, and me. In the end, the "Kili Bowl," as it became commonly known, far exceeded my expectations and those of Chris Creighton. It literally changed the lives of countless individuals involved, who came from three uniquely different parts of the world: Iowa, Mexico, and Tanzania.

1

One Man's Dream—the Commitment of Many

No, or the answer "no," doesn't necessarily mean it's a bad idea or a bad concept, it may just mean that it hasn't been presented to the right person in the right way at the right time.

Coach Chris Creighton

I believe life is all about commitment. The more you commit, and the stronger your commitment is, the goal you've set is no longer just an idle talking point. This was a commitment I had made to a head coach I aspired to be more like, and to an athletic director I was growing to know and respect more every day, and to eighty young men who totally trusted me. A man's word, his commitment, is his spirit, his essence as a man.

In the summer of 2009, Chris Creighton had been the HeadFootball Coach at Drake University for just one season, and was busily involved in recruiting events on campus. Throughout his first year, Chris worked closely with his Athletic Director, Sandy Hatfield Clubb, on various team initiatives focused around five specific program goals:

1. Academic Excellence
2. Being Your Best
3. Family
4. Fun
5. Impact Men

Throughout this time, he had shared his ultimate professional dream with her, to take one of his football teams to Africa to climb Mount Kilimanjaro, the tallest freestanding mountain in the world with an elevation of 19,341 ft (5,895 m).

Chris's first head coaching job in 1997 was at Ottawa University, an NAIA (National Association of Intercollegiate Athletics) program in Kansas. During his four years there, as part of his leadership series, he decided that he would take his staff and seniors during the summer to climb Pikes Peak in Colorado. Each climb was memorable and impactful. When he started coaching at NCAA (National Collegiate Athletic Association) schools such as Wabash College, rules prohibited him from continuing to organize his coaches and players to climb mountains as a team, though he always challenged them to do it on their own. Throughout the years many accepted the challenge, but Coach Creighton knew that he still wanted to do more for his players.

He was motivated to create the ultimate team building experience that would not only change the way his players worked together as a team, but one that would also give them an unforgettable life experience and a way to become "impact men." An experience that would enable his team to serve the community selflessly, to bring a positive influence into the lives of those involved in the football program, and to carry that positive influence on with them into their homes, businesses, families and ultimately in the world, long after they graduated. Now this is a football coach for whom parents would want their sons to play!

Chris had done a little bit of research about American football in Tanzania before coming to me with the idea, asking me to help him achieve his dream. Through his inquiries, and much to his surprise, he discovered there had been no real games in Africa. He searched for any official game he could find on African soil, but came up with nothing, aside from a couple of military base games organized by the troops. Now he was fired up!

This fact added a burst of excitement to the dream, as it would allow his team to play in the very first official football game on African soil! Coach Creighton could take his team to climb Mt. Kilimanjaro and, to top it off, provide his team the opportunity to give back to the Tanzanian children through community service work. He felt that this would be the opportunity of a lifetime for his young athletes, and exactly what he had been searching for.

When Chris was sixteen years old, he joined 'Teens Missions International,' traveling to Haiti for one and a half months on a mission project, living in tents and helping to build a farm. "A very intense experience," as he recalls. Then, during the second semester of his junior year at Kenyon College he did a semester abroad in Ecuador, "Another awesome experience." As head coach, his vision had always been to make playing football in his program one of the most incredible experiences of a young man's life. Based on his personal experiences overseas, he felt "spending time in another country is one way to make an experience incredible."

While coaching at Wabash College in 2003 his team traveled with my company, Global Football, to Switzerland and Austria. This was a good trip for him, a nice experiential learning opportunity, but he didn't feel it had the true impact on his players that he was looking for, the kind that being in a developing country had had on his life. So in 2006 he and I brainstormed on their next trip. He wanted to play in a less developed country, and include a community service work component to the tour.

We decided to take the team to Panama, a country I was familiar with from previous work with local high school age teams, as well as having had some college friends at Notre Dame from the Central American nation. We broke the traditional mold of football travel by going to Panama to do significant service work with the local people, in addition to playing a football game against the Panamanian Senior National Team. During the eight-day trip, we rode in dugout boats in the Panama Canal, learned about the rich Spanish and indigenous histories, marveled at the wildlife, played some football and enjoyed the expansive beaches.

Most importantly, the team spent three days working in the steep, wet Pacific highlands on a cooperative farm which a number of native families shared. The boys planted maize, furrowed land for beans and dug out a ten meter diameter circular tilapia fish pond that would thrive on land that previously seemed to grow only rocks. It was an amazing trip and seemed to be just what Coach Creighton had been in search of.

In the back of his mind, though, he still had his eyes set on Africa. To him that would be the Big Kahuna, the ultimate experience. Throughout his first year at Drake University, he had always talked to recruits about the overseas trips he had taken with his Wabash teams and his desire to one day take a team to Africa.

That summer of '09 when Chris shared his dream with Sandy, she related to him that she had summited Kilimanjaro with her father for his birthday about seventeen years earlier. As Sandy had already been there, she couldn't wait to go back. "Once you go to East Africa, you will find a way to go back." Not only did she want to return, but she was also eager to do everything in her power to help Coach Creighton be the role model for what other coaches at Drake could be. So, she told him, "Chris, we have to make this happen!"

Sandy, who lives every day with a level of passion rarely seen, was enthusiastic to help make this dream come to life and offered to do all she could to help him. However, before they could get the ball rolling on this event they had to take a few preliminary steps, like receiving approval from various members in the University including the President, the Provost and the Board of Trustees. Another key organization they had to speak with was the NCAA to receive their approval, and to ensure they were properly informed as to all of the governing body's rules associated with international travel for a Division I football team.

After speaking to the NCAA, which supported the event, though did not express much confidence that it could be successfully executed, Sandy went on to discuss the idea with the Drake president, Dr. David Maxwell. He embraced the idea from the beginning. Immediately he understood that the event would help define the mission of the institution, that of being an exceptional learning environment. Also, how through athletics Drake University worked to help young people realize their dreams and stretch those dreams to new places. He asked if he could go on the trip as well, to which Sandy replied, "Are you kidding? Absolutely! That would be amazing!" It was imperative that President Maxwell gave his personal backing, as there were some skeptics in other parts of the University who liked the idea but were apprehensive about the cost, potential liability and logistics. Sandy didn't let these issues worry her, as she totally believed she and Chris would get it done, overcoming any items that might stand in the way.

She had been to Tanzania and knew the quirkiness and concerns about being in a developing country, but also had complete confidence in the local tour guide we would soon hire and trust intimately, Frank Mella, whom she had gotten to know on her previous trip. This was all done before Chris attended the annual American Football Coaches Association convention in January of 2010 and shared his dream with me. I was hooked from the start, honored that I was asked to join their team and to serve as leader of the project.

To make this dream a reality, I had to get a basic understanding of what we wanted to accomplish, and prioritize the action points before

I could start planning the event and putting all of my "teams" together. The very first task at hand was to find another team to play. Due of my experience organizing international football events, I understand that NCAA rules are always the first thing I check when working with American colleges. In order for Drake University, a Division I-AA nonscholarship level school to play an off-season game internationally, they must play a foreign team on foreign soil during a university vacation period. Satisfied that we would be following the NCAA rules, my first challenge, and goal became finding a foreign opponent. Simple enough to say.

I was so excited about the prospect that had been presented to me by Coach Creighton that I immediately wanted to reach out to some international contacts I thought might have an interest, but first I needed to figure out some basics, such as pricing. From my initial research, I figured that, including flights and land cost, the travel was going to run around $4,000 USD per person. A somewhat daunting figure as many unknowns remained and we had never, during my fifteen years of running Global Football, charged that much for a tour. Also, this figure did not include any of my pre-trip costs, fluctuations in currency, or profit margins, and a presumption that flight costs would remain stable over the next eighteen months' time. Coach Creighton was planning for the game to take place in late May 2011, right after school let out for the summer, when colleges traditionally travel for experiential learning opportunities and to play this type of game.

Now that I had an estimated price, and tour dates, I was ready to begin reaching out to my international contacts. Surely someone would quickly grasp the opportunity Coach Creighton, Sandy, and I envisioned. Who wouldn't want to join us and make history by playing in the first American football game on the African continent? I would soon find out!

My first outreach was to the Tec de Monterrey University in Monterrey, Mexico through Coach Frank González and his Director of Student Affairs. Monterrey boasts the largest campus among the twenty-three Tec de Monterrey college system schools. They have also been the most successful American football team in Mexico for decades.

At one point, when both the private and public league schools played together, they had won nine out of ten National Championships! I had gotten to know Coach Frank very well over the years working with him on two post-season events, the 'Tazón de Azteca' and 'Tazón de Estrellas' all-star games featuring top NCAA Division III players and their Mexican peers. I believed this African project was just too big of a dream to try to explain via e-mail. So I made the trip to Monterrey, Mexico to meet with him, information in hand, fully expecting that he would quickly grasp the vision and jump on board.

Coach González listened intently to my presentation as I explained the dream Coach Creighton had brought to me, as well as some of the realities it would take to make this happen. I seemed to have sparked his interest a bit as he took me to his Director of Student Affairs for the campus, who oversaw athletics as well as international exchange and study. I presented the entire idea again to the two of them, and they responded that they were interested, but needed just a little bit of time to think.

However, as I returned home, I had a bad feeling about this. The dangerous thing about someone taking their time to mull over an opportunity of this magnitude is that there are too many reasons *not* to do it. Saying no is a safe decision.

That is exactly what happened. He came back a few weeks later telling me all of the reasons why this would not be of interest to them, at this time…perhaps in the future after someone else had broken ground and shown that it could actually work. I was bummed!

I became concerned that this might become a common response. You see, like Frank, many of my contacts are football guys first and foremost, and this event was so much more than purely football. From that moment in February until July 2010, I spent most all of my time and effort on finding a second team for this event, a partner and opponent for the Drake Bulldogs.

Until this point in my career, I had produced football events in nineteen different countries. So naturally, I started reviewing my broad list of international contacts to find a prospective team. I started with my closest allies, sent each team and country contact a letter of invitation, an overview of the event, as well as an idea of how the community service element would be included. I added information on the safari and the mountain expedition, gave them all of the positive reasons why this would work and why Drake University was so fired up about it. Then I followed up with a personal phone call.

For months, just when I would begin to get discouraged, Coach Creighton would call periodically and ask me how things were going. I would tell him that I was still working on it, that I would definitely find somebody for him. I just didn't know who that someone was quite yet.

The following is a list of most of the countries and teams around the world that turned me down, basically everybody with a football program at the time:

Japan—Coach Shinzo Yamada, a former NFL Europe player and current coach of the IBM Big Blue Team in Japan's Summer Pro X League. A highly motivated individual, he and I had worked together to produce the Notre Dame Japan Bowl in 2009. He seemed intrigued and bounced the idea around to a few people but just didn't find any real interest at that time, from either the Japanese universities or the corporate semi-pro X League.

Germany—Federation President Robert Huber oversaw numerous quality teams, the most in Europe, many with solid financial backing. Being in Europe, the flights would be easier and cheaper to reach Africa. But the game wasn't what they were looking for.

Italy—FIDAF, the Italian American Football Federation, and the country we travel to most often with teams, with innovative leadership. Didn't work for them either.

Australia—American football was very well organized there, and I had many dear friends, led by Paul Manera, whom I contacted, but it wasn't something they were interested in.

Sweden—The IFAF (International Federation of American Football) President, Tommy Wiking lives in his native homeland of Sweden. The event seemed to fit the IFAF initiative of expanding American football as broadly as possible, so I thought they might have a bit more interest, but he told me they couldn't do it.

Finland—Another well organized league, led by the energetic Roope Noronen. Yet another dead end.

Austria—Every year since 2001 we had worked together to put on the Vienna Charity Bowl, produced in an extremely professional manner by Karl Wurm and Alfred Neugebauer. I believe this is the best annual football event in Europe. But they were a no go.

France—The dynamic president of the French American Football Federation is Marco Soumah, whose family is from Africa, so he had a personal interest. In the end though, they just could not do it.

Denmark—No thanks.

Russia—We had done a spectacular youth event there in 1999, so I thought maybe, but no.

Spain—Great friend there in Marcos Guirles, former NFL Europe coach, but "Lo siento".

Holland—Even with direct KLM flights from Amsterdam to Tanzania, they chose not to do it. We ended up flying both Drake and Mexico CONADEIP through Amsterdam to Kilimanjaro Airport in Tanzania.

Panama—Years back, Guillermo Suárez had brought his junior team to Atlanta for the NFL Global Jr Championship and there were some reliable funding sources there for football…but nope.

Canada—I thought, well, what about Canada, as I knew all the key football guys in Quebec and this might just work for them. They were well organized, and played in the schools just like Mexico and Japan (club teams seemed to be harder to get organized and put together). I had worked with some of these coaches for the past eleven years as they had been part of the NFL Global Junior Championship events. These were a showcase for teenage players around the world, an idea I created alongside the Super Bowl program in 1997, with the event running through 2008. I spoke to the various Canadian coaches at different universities, but they all said the event wouldn't work for them either.

Mexico Pumas—I returned to Mexico City to meet with the most successful public university in the country, the National University Pumas, knowing how competitive they had become with Tec de Monterrey. But no, gracias.

The responses and excuses were always the same, "Wow, this sounds like a great idea, but why should we go all the way to Tanzania to play football?"

The reasons against it were clear: the costs were high, there had never been a game there, hardly anyone knew or seemed to care where Tanzania was, worries of safety, such a monumental project, to name just a few. Finding a willing opponent and partner, I had discovered, wasn't going to be an easy task.

In any aspect of life, for those who do not have the vision or ability to do something daring, something brand new, it is always easier to say no than to consider the possibilities of how to say yes and get it done. Perhaps teams were afraid because nobody else had ever done it? Maybe there was a valid reason nobody had ever atattempted to do it? I was quickly discovering several reasons why not, but didn't want to hear them!

The most important factors in favor of finding an opponent and making this happen, the compelling reasons I wanted to do it, and why Coach Creighton and his Athletic Director, Sandy Hatfield Clubb, were so fired up about it were very clear:

- Just one, or, in this case, two teams could ever be the first to play an official game of American Football in Tanzania, let alone the continent of Africa.
- Never had an American football team, or two of them, climbed to the summit of Mt. Kilimanjaro.
- This would *rock the world* of each student athlete who would work in the orphanages, hospitals, schools, and health clinics of Tanzania.

To me, it is a colossal thing to be the first to do something. I have accomplished a lot of wonderful things in my life, *but I've never been able to say that I was the first*. Also, my primary goal in Global Football is to give amateur student athletes a chance to travel and compete, to experience other cultures with their teammates, to serve those peoples, and to learn through doing. We achieve this many times each year through demonstrating and sharing the players' skills and understanding of American football with a multitude of cultures, in countries across the globe.

To Coach Chris Creighton, the most important and critical element of this event was the service aspect. It appears that the typically American view of community service is becoming more and more a key component in international travel, which I am delighted to witness. The act of service provides those of us who are blessed, simply by birth, to share our time and energy and to give back to the world and those less fortunate.

Tanzania is a country where only a quarter of the population has access to adequate sanitation facilities, where only half of the population enjoys the benefit of clean water, where only twothirds of households use at least one insecticide-treated bed net to help prevent malaria, the leading killer of Tanzanian children under the age of five; and where nearly 12 percent of the children are orphaned. Tanzania seemed like the perfect country for which to provide some badly needed community service.

From the moment Coach Creighton spoke to me at the AFCA Convention in January, I spent every day of every week targeting and talking to potential opponents, in addition to planning the event logistics. I was working hard to find the other team and, come the end of July, six months after Chris presented me with his dream; still no viable prospect had emerged. In the meantime, he would call, and we would work on planning the details, itineraries and pricing for the trip. While addressing all these details was critical, none of it mattered unless we found an opponent for the game.

With most Global Football trips, I typically send the US teams over to the countries where they play a local American football club, the national all-star team, or in some cases, a university team. Obviously this couldn't happen in Tanzania where they had barely heard of the game of American football, and certainly did not have an organized team to play.

Despite the numerous obstacles, I just couldn't give up, primarily because Coach Creighton was so passionate about it, but also because I had given him and his players my word that I would get it done. I wouldn't give up until I found their opponent; a willing partner with the same vision and commitment.

While I was searching the globe to find another team and making plans with Coach Creighton, Drake University had made tremendous progress on their end. Coach had immediately begun to put his own support team together. Right after he had returned from the coaches' convention he had his first squad meeting of the year. He made a quick announcement about winter workouts and then couldn't wait any longer. He was barely able to contain himself as he told his players that they were going to Africa, would play the first-ever American football game on the continent, followed by community service projects, and to top it all off, they would climb to the summit of Mt. Kilimanjaro.

After calming down a bit, he explained how this would happen. Yes, they would have to raise a substantial amount of money, and, yes, we still had to find somebody to play, but everyone would work together to make sure it happen. So while he got his players raring to go, the broader "Team Drake," Sandy, and others began their fundraising initiatives.

In May of 2010, just before school let out for the summer, I made a trip to Des Moines, Iowa to meet with Chris, Sandy, the players and a number of the other people involved. I was able to watch all their eyes light up personally, as I made a presentation in the auditorium covering the myriad of aspects of the event. As I gave them the basic outline of the sixteen-day itinerary, the hows, whats and wheres, including some of the climbing initiatives, I could see that they were all mentally prepared and eagerly awaiting this opportunity.

I had also identified the cost per individual for the event. To this point I had not ever been to Tanzania but had done extensive research on it as well as collected valuable resources from people like Sandy, who had been there. She was also able to put me in contact with Del Christensen, the Executive Director of a nonprofit organization called the Iowa Resource for International Service (IRIS) whom we would end up working with on the multi-faceted community service portion of the trip. The Iowa team was coming together nicely. Near the end of the presentation, one of the student athletes raised his hand and said thoughtfully, "Thank you, Coach Patrick, for showing this to us, we are all fired up about it, but who are we going to play?"

There were about eighty young men in the room who were all bright-eyed, serious student athletes enrolled in a great university trying to improve their lives and the lives of others. I could clearly sense their excitement. Right then I made another huge commitment in front of all of them when I boldly stated, "You know…I don't have your opponent just yet, but I *will* find one."

With that promise and the one I had made back in January to Coach Creighton, there was no way I could go against my word and let all of them down. Finding an opponent was just another piece in the puzzle, albeit a hugely significant one, of making such a huge dream like this come to life.

I returned home to Texas with renewed hope and spirit. Coach Creighton and I had a lengthy talk following the team meeting which was direct and friendly, with great respect for one another. I discussed with him all of the people who had turned me down thus far, and we reviewed more options for finding an opponent. I reiterated my commitment—I would not let him down!

I proceeded to spend the entire month of June talking to other teams, even those that from my experience seemed a bit more farfetched. There was a British group I knew through my NFL Europe work, but they chose not to take it on, as well. I also spoke to the folks in Spain and Denmark, again. They weren't the best football teams in the world, but they were eager, organized people. Neither of those teams decided to commit.

I even tried a different tact, reaching out to a former Notre Dame classmate of mine, Mike Whalen, with whom I had stayed in touch with over the years. He was a main player in producing events for the United States military in the Middle East. Mike handled the big Coaches Tour in support of our troops, every year to that region through his Morale Entertainment Foundation. My thought was that we may be able to put together a US military team which could play against Drake, thereby reducing overall costs, since they would already be in the area. It would also be a great way to promote our military and the work they do while providing some entertainment for our troops who participated. We took the idea in a number of different directions until Mike got in touch with some of his contacts in the Pentagon. They indicated that a strict rule had been enacted a few years back not allowing those on active duty to play tackle football. Obviously, we couldn't go all the way to Tanzania and play touch or flag football. Unfortunately, that idea turned into yet another dead end.

I can't say I never felt disheartened. It became exceedingly frustrating as I contacted many dynamic, get 'er done types of people from around the world, only to be turned down. It just seemed that nobody else was able to totally grasp the vision as Chris Creighton and I had.

Still, I couldn't imagine making the dreaded phone call to Chris saying that we had to give up on his dream, which had become the dream of so many, because I couldn't find an opponent. I had told him, and his team, I would do it. Giving up was simply not an option. I just had not yet found the right person.

"No" doesn't necessarily mean it's a bad idea or a bad concept, it just means it hasn't been presented to the right person, in the right way, at the right time.

Finally, in July, I found the man who shared the vision with Chris Creighton and me, and ultimately would share this journey with us. His name was Dr. Enrique Ramos, Director of Student Affairs for the Tec de Monterrey system in Mexico. He was based in Monterrey and was responsible for athletics, international study, exchange students, and every aspect of student life that did not deal with academics directly for the twenty-three Tec campuses. His Monterrey campus director was part of my initial meeting and proposal to Coach Frank months ago, and they had turned me down.

Enrique, however, was able to see far beyond the reasons not to do it. He quickly embraced the value this project would have for each student athlete who traveled, for those in Tanzania the travelers would come in contact with, and for the Tec de Monterrey University itself. This idea, this trip, would demonstrate exactly what Enrique believed the spirit of Tec was. Through his vision and commitment, by taking this dream on as his own, he made it possible for everyone to share this experience.

View from the Summit

Every time I think back to the Kili Bowl event, it becomes frighteningly clear how easy it would have been to just give up on the idea. Then I consider all the people who would not have lived the experience, had I listened to all who told me no. Commitment is what drove me to keep forging ahead, especially in the quest to find a willing opponent and partner.

Commitment! My word to Coach Creighton, to Sandy Clubb, and to the entire Drake football team that I would find that other team. Commitment is what separates those who think of ideas from those who act upon them, the men from the boys.

2

Mexico Joins the Team

It is critical that the Dream not only belong to the dreamer, as it will take a TEAM effort to accomplish the stated goals. It must become THEIR dream also, THEIR story to tell, THEIR sense of commitment and feeling of pride.

CONADEIP player

Dr. Enrique Ramos became the Kili Bowl missionary within Mexico, carrying the message far and wide. These days he and I often look back and reflect on just how far "out on a limb" he truly was, being initially the one individual in the world, outside of Drake University and Global Football, who believed in this lofty project! I am sure there were some lonely moments for him, some doubts, but in the end he persevered and succeeded. He took on Coach Creighton's dream, my dream and extended it across the top private university system of Mexico. Quite simply, it was his belief and commitment that allowed the event to occur.

American Football has longstanding roots in Mexico. As early as 1896, a group of Mexicans who had studied in the United States brought the sport back home, organizing friendly games. The sport grew throughout the 1920s when it became popular in universities across the country. Over one hundred twenty-five years later, what began as a friendly game of flag football has grown into one of the largest markets for the sport outside of the United States. Best estimates of participation indicate that over a hundred thousand players, ages 5 to 23, participate in the sport, a fact mostly unknown outside of Mexico.

Nearly all of the private colleges and universities play in the CONADEIP organization (The Student National Sports Commission of Private Institutions). In recent decades, Tec de Monterrey, Monterrey campus, has been the most successful team in Mexico, dominating the league as it did the larger public and private schools' ONEFA league prior to 2008.

Most of my recent efforts in Mexico have been with CONADEIP as the majority of my dealings over the past decade had been with the Tec de Monterrey schools, whose members comprise the largest number of private colleges. I have always enjoyed this relationship because they were clear about what they could do, what they could not, and when they would do it. As I have found from my history of producing games worldwide, this trait is not always prevalent.

The men I had worked with were dedicated to improving their football players, their teams, and their reputations as quality institutions of higher learning. To them, football and athletics were essential components of college life, but they were not the ultimate reason to attend their schools. These were exceptionally acclaimed institutes of higher learning, proud of their students' successes, their alumni esteemed positions and their global presence. The Tec campuses, of which there are currently twenty-three universities and thirty-two *prepa* or high schools, are spread out across Mexico, with Monterrey in the northern state of Nuevo Leon serving as its hub.

Dr. Enrique Ramos, who earned his doctorate from the University of Arizona, is the Director of Student Affairs for the overall Tec de Monterrey system. Working under him is the Student Affairs Director on each campus. In this role, all student activities report to him, including athletics and their coaches, international student exchange programs as well as the international student studies.

A native of the Mexican state of Durango, Enrique studied at Tec as an undergraduate and for his Masters Degree at the Monterrey Campus before going to the US to earn his Doctorate in Administration. He is thoroughly fluent in English, gregarious and comfortable in most any situation. Enrique is highly respected by both coaches and academicians and completely dedicated to the betterment of his students and the university overall.

I had the chance to work closely with Enrique to create and develop the post-season Tazón de Estrellas (Bowl of Stars) game in 2009. Throughout that year, I worked with him on setting the game's parameters, creating guidelines and budgets, and ultimately producing a highly successful event, which was staged on the campus of Tec de Monterrey CEM, on the outskirts of Mexico City. During that time I found him to be an exceptionally dedicated individual with a wonderful blend of wit, humor and sincere caring. I enjoyed working with him as we seemed to have similar work habits and styles.

In late July 2010, he had given me a call to talk about the next Tazón de Estrellas which would be staged in December. After the call, I was relieved to know that he was continuing to work on the Tazón, an event that had become highly anticipated on both sides of the border. In America, this game serves as the most esteemed post-season opportunity for NCAA Division III seniors to showcase their talents and enjoy one last game. In Mexico, the game provides a chance for their top college stars to go up against Americans and prove the high quality of football being played south of the border. Enrique, fortunately, was eager to see this annual event continue.

I was thrilled by this call and his exuberance, but as I sat in my Texas office, I remained terribly frustrated by the fact that I couldn't find another team for Tanzania which I needed to help fulfill Coach Creighton's dream. I also knew that Sandy had stated an ultimatum, saying if another team was not found before summer football camp, the first week of August, the event would have to be postponed.

As I sat there and thought about the December Tazón, I suddenly had an awakening. This could be perfect! What if I got Enrique excited about taking a CONADEP All-Star team to Tanzania? He was obviously a man who liked to do big, positive things for his university and their students. He was well respected by his superiors, an eager proponent of branding the Monterrey Tec name and image globally. This could be perfect!

I had been told no by nearly every football-playing nation and leader around the world. In fact, I had been turned down by Enrique's Tec Monterrey head coach months prior. Maybe this time, possibly, this man would really understand the dream, capture the vision, and sense the opportunity where none had previously?

I promptly drafted him an email telling him that I had already spoken to Coach Frank at the University campus in Monterrey, and had been turned down but that this event was much bigger than just one campus. I went on to explain how this could bring worldwide visibility to the whole CONADEIP system, creating branding for them, separate from that of other Mexican Universities and ONEFA, which was very much needed at the time. The CONADEIP league had existed as a separate entity for decades but only as a main player in other sports, never in football, until the separation from ONEFA in 2008. So it was important for CONADEIP to have visibility in football both within Mexico as well as internationally.

Most importantly, though, this historic event in Tanzania would provide an international educational experience for their student athletes, as well as the vital service work, which had become more and more an integral part of the curriculum at the CONDADEIP schools. I sent an email, and then proceeded to call him a couple of days after to provide clarification and explain my email in more depth. He obviously had questions, and even though he seemed a little guarded, Enrique clearly was intrigued, even somewhat enthusiastic about the opportunity. When I hung up I remember clenching my fist and pumping it with a big yes! At that moment, I realized, after seven months of searching for an opponent, I may have found the ideal partner for Drake University in the CONADEIP League All-Stars from Mexico.

Over the next few days, Enrique and I corresponded numerous times by email and phone, discussing many facets of the trip. I could tell he thought it was a good idea but possibly wasn't sure about the feasibility. I kept up my politely pestering behavior, about which Enrique later would tell me, "If you hadn't called every week, I don't think it really would have happened." We were considering a unique concept, a massive undertaking in fundraising and logistics, but something that I had worked through in my brain and on paper so many times that it had become second nature to me. He quickly grasped the myriad of complexities, understood the reasons why, and dismissed those reasons why not.

While Enrique was ready to extend this possibility to his student athletes, he still had a few major obstacles to cross. First and foremost, he had to present the idea to his boss, Dr. Carlos Mijares, the Vice President of Academics at Tec de Monterrey. Following their initial meeting, I awaited Enrique's reply for a few anxious days. Enrique had explained to Dr. Mijares, a physically slight, but mentally huge man with a wonderful breadth of worldly knowledge, that this was an idea worthy of his time and energy. It would be incredibly valuable to the institution and the student athletes.

Dr. Mijares loved the idea! He appreciated that the event would offer two of the main educational objectives to their student athletes:

1. It would provide a formal curricular and co-curricular international experience for the students.

2. It would grant them an opportunity for social responsibility and citizenship through community service.

The other part that caught the attention of Dr. Mijares was the fact that this event was not only going to be about football, but it would start an important relationship with another institution in which they could exchange ideas. Tec de Monterrey is known worldwide as an extraordinary institution of higher learning. They have been able to achieve this standard through developing relationships with other universities throughout the world that are known for specific areas of expertise, and offering their students and faculty a chance to learn from those schools to better themselves. Tec was specifically interested in the Intercollegiate Athletics program at Drake, and this event would serve as the perfect icebreaker for the two universities to form a strong bond for the future.

After securing Dr. Mijares's support, a key step, Enrique had to persuade the individual Student Affairs Directors at the various campuses, along with the athletic directors and football coaches. He needed their support and involvement in order to make this possible. In turn, they had to find support from their student athletes. In addition, he had to lead the effort to secure the needed funding for the entire Mexican contingent. Let's just say he had quite a bit of work to do, a chore he gladly accepted and persevered through with extraordinary commitment.

Enrique scheduled a trip to Dallas at the end of July to meet with me and a few other people concerning the Tazón de Estrellas. I was eager to receive a definitive answer regarding the Kili Bowl. The only obstacle to Enrique saying yes was a couple of his colleagues who were not 100 percent on board. In the last month, he had presented the idea to his Student Affairs Directors at each of the six key football campuses. Initially, all of them were not quite convinced that the project was worth the time, money, and energy it would take.

Enrique went on to tell them that this event "would be a unique opportunity for us to really provide the kids with a life changing experience." He also said, "The easiest path for all of us is to say no.

All I have to do is send an email or make a phone call, and we are out of it. Try not to be that way, because we ask our students to do many things that sometimes we are not willing to do ourselves. I understand that I don't have the age or strength to do a lot of things, but I have the will. We must not pass up the opportunity to transcend the lives of our students, as they will remember this for the rest of their lives."

This small speech changed the minds of four out of the six directors, but by the time his Dallas trip came around, there were still two on the fence. In his hotel lobby, as we met, I asked if he would call the last two to confirm their participation and give the event the go ahead. Enrique proceeded to call and convince each director of the importance and value of the project, stressing that together they would be able to get over the hurdles.

Once he received confirmation from the last two directors, we hurriedly called Coach Creighton to share the good news. Preparing for camp, Creighton was in meetings all day and did not receive the message until late that evening. The second he heard the news he immediately tried, to no avail, to call me back. He wanted to share the good news with somebody, so he called his wife. No answer. He tried to find one of his coaches, but no one was available. So there he was standing on the catwalk of the aged red brick field house at Drake University, alone. As Coach Creighton describes, "It was one of those moments where it was between me and God. It was as if God was saying, don't talk to Patrick, don't talk to the coaches, don't talk to your wife; thank me, because I'm in this with you."

Later that night, Enrique and I were able to get hold of Coach Creighton, and he expressed his heartfelt gratitude toward us. To this day, Enrique "can still feel Chris' excitement and how thankful he was for all of the people who were dedicated to providing our students and us with a life changing experience." This moment seemed to mark the true reality of the event coming to life. We all firmly believed, at that exact point in time that the Kili Bowl was going to happen. It was a true, deep feeling of satisfaction.

In early October, Dr. Ramos, Dr. Mijares, and I traveled to Drake University on Homecoming Weekend for our formal announcement meeting. It had become wonderfully obvious to both Drake and CONADEIP that this was not just to be a singular event involving football, service work and a mountain climb; but rather this was to begin a relationship between and among visionary educators and universities from America and Mexico. This event would truly become something historical in the world of higher education. Upon my arrival at Drake, I was struck by how professional Sandy and the others were in their approach to their visitors. The entire three-day weekend was perfectly scripted, allowing Dr. Ramos and Dr. Mijares to meet, share time with, and best understand the Drake community and its mission.

As it turned out, and not surprisingly, Enrique and Sandy quickly connected on many levels. They had very similar visions in terms of thinking on a much larger plane about sports. They were also two people completely devoted to their professions while showing great respect and admiration for others. Coach Creighton was busy preparing his team for the football game that weekend against Davidson College, but he took plenty of time to meet with everybody and made us all feel welcome.

Our entire group visited with President David Maxwell, who was planning to make the journey to Tanzania along with his two sons. His support proved to be essential in the overall event. The Provost of Drake, Dr. Michael Renner was most cordial as we sat in his office, in the nearly regal administration building, discussing a multitude of non-athletic components and opportunities this would bring to both the schools.

We enjoyed lunch with Dr. Thomas Westbrook and Dr. Debra Bishop, both of whom would be involved with teaching the Drake leadership course prior to and throughout the entire Tanzania experience. The title of the course was "Leading with Emotional Intelligence: The Tanzania Experience," and seemed to capture the imagination of our Mexican allies as well. This course would not be mandatory, but highly recommended for all the Drake student athletes who were going on the trip. Discussions arose for ideas of doing something similar in Mexico. There was talk of future student, student athlete and faculty exchanges, and about shared distance learning. I sat there in amazement as these talented educators from different countries, so much more learned than me, sought out creative ways to work together for common goals. From that first meeting to today the relationship between the two universities continues to evolve, due to the vision of their leaders.

A memorable photo was staged and taken with the core team of organizers holding the Global Kilimanjaro Bowl banner: Coach Chris Creighton, Sandy Hatfield Clubb, Dr. Javier Mijares, Dr. Enrique Ramos, Del Christensen of IRIS, and me, all sporting our high altitude younger optic sunglasses. Game on!

The next day, we attended the Drake Homecoming game, a victory for the Bulldogs. As I stood on the sidelines just before kickoff, gazing at the crisp blue sky, offset by a similar blue trim on the Drake players' uniforms, I took a deep breath, and for the first time allowed myself to believe that this was really going to happen! I felt a sincere sense of gratitude to Coach Creighton for bringing his dream to me, as well as a deep feeling of thanks to Enrique Ramos for believing in this 'crazy gringo' and his wacky notion to stage a game in Africa.

My mind also drifted back to January 1, 1971, at the Cotton Bowl in Dallas, Texas, on a similarly pristine day when I was there dressed in tight gold pants, white jersey and blazing gold helmet, about to play the University of Texas and halt their thirty game winning streak. I recalled my nervous, though positive emotions of that day, appreciating that while I was not on the star level of starting QB Joe Theismann, I did play a role on this highly successful team. I reminisced about how my college career had been quietly cut short by a shoulder injury on the Cartier practice field, and that my NFL dreams were instantly dashed, causing me for many years to feel somewhat cheated by fate. Now, some forty years later, there I was, once again standing on a football sideline, about to undertake a monumental and far grander "game effort"—the Global Kilimanjaro Bowl in Tanzania.

I stood among my new teammates, my friends from Drake and CONADEIP, thinking about the journey we were about to embark upon and the total commitment we had now made. It felt just like pregame—so much to do, so much to execute, and knowing that, as a team, we would be able to prevail over any opponent.

Once that gathering in October was held, once those amazingly dedicated men and women got to know one another personally, I felt that the event was set in stone and was going to occur on a grand scale!

The "teams" started building in Mexico. Enrique began to put his organizational team together which included a young man named Iván Loredo. An expert climber himself, Iván became Enrique's coordinator for all of the climbing related activities. Also joining the 'team' was a highly motivated young lady, Zuleika de Alba, who helped find sponsors to raise money for the CONADEIP team and others. Carmelo Ramírez became Enrique's right-hand man for operations, a skilled and personable longtime friend of Enrique who worked in his office on a daily basis. He would ultimately organize all of the lists of people, needs, and flight arrangements. Carmelo also spearheaded the coordination of people at the various campuses, a monumental task. He too would make the trip to Tanzania and successfully climb Mt. Kilimanjaro!

While everybody got on board, there were always concerns in the back of their minds about varying aspects of the trip, especially the funding. As Dr. Mijares put it, "We were very optimistic, and as it usually happens, when you are convinced and believe in the value of any difficult project, you will always overcome the challenges."

View from the Summit

It's one thing to develop an idea and run with it, organizing a team of close acquaintances to help achieve your goal. It is quite another to broadly expand your idea and take it truly global, to seek out, find, and influence individuals who will go out of their comfort zones and buy into the idea or concept, with total commitment and enthusiasm. I found that person in Dr. Enrique Ramos. He honestly went out on a limb—way out. He committed to me, as I committed to Coach Creighton. This person is out there, but not easily found. If it were easy, everybody would do it!

3

In God's Hands from the Beginning

As Dr. Steve Meyer read the article in the *Des Moines Register* about the Drake football team going to Tanzania, he was sure there was a misprint. There was no way anybody would take two entire football teams from the Americas to play in Tanzania. "It just isn't done; never has been done. But if it is going to happen, I have to get on board and be a part of it."

Dr. Steve Meyer

I am, at times, astonished to know that at the end of the day we somehow got all of the right people needed to be involved in this event and make it a success—top quality, dedicated, motivated people from Iowa, Mexico, Tanzania, and elsewhere. I would love to say it was all due to my great planning and insight, but in reality, most of it was just a matter of working through my personal contacts, inquiring about their contacts, and presenting a compelling explanation of the dream!

A more accurate way to look at it was that, in large part, this was "in God's hands" from the very beginning. So many key people came to the project, virtually out of nowhere, that this was not just luck or happenstance. There was a bigger power involved, as Chris and Sandy noted from the start, and this was proven correct throughout the course of the entire event. While I consider myself a Christian and practicing Catholic, boosted by sixteen years of Catholic education, my faith pales in comparison to that of Coach Creighton and Sandy Hatfield Clubb. They believed all along that, with God's help, the Global Kilimanjaro Bowl would work; without His direction it had no chance. Every step along the way their faith proved to be well founded.

As my Irish mother often noted, "God helps those who help themselves." I was planning to execute the Kili Bowl whether we had some of the contacts we eventually made along the way on board or not. But having friends like Dr. Meyer and Lazaro Nyalandu really helped to make the event a successful, momentous occasion for all, while making my job so much easier. It is hard to imagine how all the pieces in Tanzania especially could have come together without their direction and assistance.

During the summer and autumn of 2010, months before the event, I made a few trips up to Des Moines to visit the people at Drake and get details of the event smoothed out. As the initial idea was that of Coach Creighton, with the total support of his athletic director, their involvement throughout the process was critical. Their faith in me and the entire project was so positive, so refreshing, it was just wonderfully energizing. One particular week, though, stands out. During those days I made a critical contact who proved vital in making the Kili Bowl a success.

Enrique Ramos was in town for the weekend football game at Drake and for meetings with various faculty and administrators so they could all get comfortable with one another. My new contact would also help support Dr. Ramos in his often lonely efforts to get all on board in Mexico!

Among our tasks that extended weekend was to appear on a local radio sports station for a talk show discussing the Kili Bowl project. Our time there proved to be a fun, engaging tenminute interview and discussion where we alternated between English and Spanish. One of the smartest things I ever did in life was to study Spanish in Guatemala during my mid-twenties. Yet another occasion where "the gringo perdido" could communicate clearly in Español, further qualifying me to work closely with my Mexican associates. Following the radio show, we all returned to Sandy's office to regroup and plan for the afternoon's battery of meetings.

As we were sitting in Sandy's office discussing plans for what needed to be done next, she received a phone call from a Dr. Steve Meyer. It seemed he had been trying to get in touch with Sandy for the past month or two, ever since a visit to his parents' house when he happened to catch the word "Tanzania" out of the corner of his eye as he walked past the local newspaper sitting on the counter. The article was about Drake University taking a trip to Tanzania to play in the first ever American football game in Africa.

Dr. Meyer was a man very familiar with the country of Tanzania. At the time I met him he had been to Tanzania about twenty-five times on medical missionary trips and still returns every six months to perform pro bono orthopedic surgeries. He was also one of the founders of STEMM (Siouxland Tanzania Educational Medical Ministries), a nonprofit organization providing locals with education, medical help, spiritual enlightenment, and now an orphanage. I cannot imagine there being another American citizen with more personal experience, dedication, and insight into Tanzania and the people there.

Back in 1995, Dr. Meyer was going through what he called a dark period in his life where he came across many uncertainties. He wasn't quite sure where to turn or how anything was going to get better. It all seemed to change the day he performed surgery on a seventeen-year old girl. He was summoned to the hospital on a 911 call and preceded to surgically insert a rod into her leg. She and her family were extremely grateful and, as her doctor, he got to know her a little bit while she was recuperating. A couple of weeks after she left the hospital, Dr. Meyer received a call from a lady in Arkansas at the Wyowam Headquarters, telling him that God had told her that he, Steve Meyers, was going to travel with her to China.

As Steve recalls, "It was amazing and I will never forget it, it was just like yesterday. The lady told me who she was and that God had just told her I was going to be coming with her to China." His immediate reaction was that an Iowa State college buddy, where he had played defensive back on the Cyclones football team a few decades ago, was playing a prank on him with a really bad accent. But this was no prank at all. The lady continued to explain that the girl whose leg he had fixed was a friend of hers and that they were planning to take a trip to bring Bibles to China. They had to have a doctor with them, but theirs had canceled two months prior, so Steve was now that doc!

He tried and tried to explain that he was not the person to go to China with them. He was suicidal and depressed, going through a divorce, starting a new practice and to top it off, he didn't even like Chinese food all that much. She still called him every day from then on for two months, until he boarded the Cathay Pacific 747 to join them on the trip across the Pacific. He still does not know how or why he made that decision, or how he ended up on the flight.

His trip to China turned out to be a life-altering event for him. He felt reborn and made a decision in his life to become an outstanding Christian. Back in Sioux City, Iowa, he had many discussions with his church pastor, Reverend Jon Gerdts, with whom he confided that he felt God wanted him to do medical mission work. Reverend Gerdts asked, "Is there any place you would like to go?" Steve knew immediately where he would end up—Africa.

Since he was a little boy growing up on a tiny farm in Northwest Iowa, he couldn't read enough books about Africa and now he knew that God had been preparing him his whole life for this new adventure.

The pastor was pleasantly surprised, for during the past year he had been praying for someone to do mission work with him in Tanzania. So together they made their way to the head pastor, to share their plans for Tanzania. The pastor explained that he couldn't even get four people to go on a weekend trip with him to Juárez, Mexico, and believed finding a group for Tanzania would be next to impossible.

Nine months later, Dr. Meyer and Reverend Gerdts took a group of twelve missionaries to Arusha, Tanzania. During the trip, the Head Pastor had suggested they get together with a young man named Lazaro Nyalandu. He explained that Lazaro had grown up in a little mud hut with twelve siblings in the Singida Region of central Tanzania, one of the most impoverished areas of the country. Through his academic achievements, he had won an award for being the number one high school graduate in the entire country of Tanzania, for which he was to receive financial aid to attend college in Iowa that coming year.

They ended up making contact with Lazaro who was extremely helpful in facilitating Steve's first trip to Tanzania. They were also put in touch with Tanzania's first lady at the time, Anna Mkapa. Through discussions, all four of them decided to found a nonprofit organization to support underprivileged children, particularly girls, who wanted to go to high school. Based on that idea, STEMM was born.

Since Steve and Lazaro's first contact with each other in 1996, a tremendous friendship was established. Lazaro went on to graduate from Wartburg College, receiving his Bachelors degree and graduating Magma Cum Laude. He was the youngest person ever elected to Parliament in Tanzania, and was Deputy Minister of Industry and Trade during the time of the Kili Bowl. Lazaro went on to serve as the Deputy Minister of Natural Resources and Tourism, and now is the Minister of Natural Resources and Tourism. He is widely considered a rising star in the political scene of Tanzania. Despite his climbing the ranks of politics, Lazaro has always seen Steve as a big brother, and they communicate often.

When I was in Sandy's office that day in October and Dr. Meyer rang her, we all decided to meet for breakfast at 6:15 a.m. the next morning where we would be able to get better acquainted with one other. Steve was coming to Des Moines from Sioux City with his young son for a youth football tournament and could meet for an early breakfast. Another stroke of luck? God works in amazing ways.

It was extremely fortunate that Steve called at that time. Not only did he have personal knowledge of football, but he pointed us towards the best medical care in Tanzania. In addition, he helped us make invaluable contacts with key politicians and leaders in the country, starting with his dear friend Lazaro. Ultimately, Dr. Meyer filled in so many of the missing pieces of the puzzle surrounding the project.

I had numerous conversations with Steve prior to January when I embarked on the second of my three scouting trips to Tanzania. It was then that through Steve I was able to be introduced to Lazaro, as well as to the municipality leaders in Arusha and Dr. Jacobson, head administrator of the Arusha Lutheran Medical Center.

Steve fully understood the medical issues involved in bringing two football teams to play a game in Tanzania. He was also deeply involved in the medical community there, a huge plus. He was thus able to make sure we were set up for any medical emergency that might ensue, noting that the only hospital in Tanzania where he would feel comfortable having our football players taken care of would be the ALMC hospital in Arusha. During my visit in January, I made a trip there to meet Dr. Jacobson, and we outlined our emergency plan in case one of the travelers became ill or injured.

Eventually, this "fortunate meeting" would also play another role in my family's life as my daughter, Xela, was able to perform six weeks of community service work at the hospital immediately following the Global Kilimanjaro Bowl, a time that transformed her life as well.

Following my time in Arusha, I traveled to Dar Es Salaam, the steamy coastal capital of Tanzania. There I stayed at the Sea Cliff Hotel where I met Lazaro for the first time. He and I had a fabulous conversation as we sat there enjoying the breeze coming in off the ocean, discussing his past history with Dr. Meyer and my expansive plans for the Kili Bowl. Steve later would tell me that he had a conversation with Lazaro the day following my introduction to him to gauge his thoughts. Lazaro's response was, "To be honest with you, when you told me that there was some guy who was going to put together an American Football game in Tanzania, I thought you were out of your mind. But after meeting Patrick, he is *the guy* who can make this happen."

In May 2011, Dr. Meyer and his son, Josh, joined us on the sideline for the face off between CONADEIP and Drake. He acted as the "Doc on the field" in case somebody had a serious injury. Even more special and impactful, the morning of the game he officially opened his own STEMM orphanage about a half hour east of Arusha, which had been a longtime dream, housing dozens of youngsters without families or housing.

Steve did not join us on the climb up Mt. Kilimanjaro. In the numerous times he had been to Tanzania, he told us he had always wanted to make the climb, but when it came down to it, he shared, "I am so overwhelmed with the thought that I could spend six days climbing Kili, or I could perform surgeries and give the gift of walking to thirty children during that time. It is an easy decision."

To help me understand why it was so compelling for him to perform surgeries rather than climb Mount Kilimanjaro, he explained his reasoning to me very succinctly. The country of Tanzania consists of forty-eight million people to which there are at most fifteen full-time orthopedic surgeons attending. Hence, there is one orthopedic surgeon for every three million people. In contrast, in the United States, there is approximately one orthopedic surgeon for every eight thousand people. If he did not perform the surgeries, it just didn't get done.

View from the Summit

It is amazing, the people who randomly pop into your life. Some just seem to come and go, others become role players, and then certain folks become so very important. I have learned since that there is a reason for this, for people coming into our lives from wildly different places, to never disregard the people we meet along the way. We never know how they will influence our lives. Without Dr. Steve Meyer, I am pretty sure the Kili Bowl would have still taken place, but it would have been so much more difficult to fill in those missing pieces. It simply would not have had the impact it did. And I would not have the much deeper appreciation for what Dr. Meyer and others like him bring to the people of Tanzania.

4

Exploring Tanzania—the Albino Baboon

In English, we use the phrase "to know," meaning to have a working knowledge of the subject. It does not indicate the depth of true personal experience with the topic, however. In Spanish the verb *conocer* indicates a person has experienced, learned firsthand, and personally knows about the subject.

In order "to know" about a land, culture, sport, wildlife, roads, flights, beauty, natural wonders, mountains, individuals, or a way of life, one cannot simply read, research, and study. There is a critical need to visit, meet, view, travel, try, communicate and do. Only this way can a leader "know" what is needed to organize, to lead in the right direction. It takes time and effort certainly, but it is the only way.

Albino baboon

The basic plan for the event was pretty simple, at least in my mind. We were going to take the Drake University football team and their followers from the heartland of America, and link them together with an all-star team from the CONADEIP Mexico league, comprised of eighteen private universities. The two teams would travel half way around the world to Tanzania to stage the first ever American football game on the continent of Africa. Simple!

Though, much more important than football was the fact that together two disparate teams would perform valuable community service work. It would be a rare opportunity for the student athletes to do some hard work for the needy citizens, and especially the children of Tanzania. They would also help provide them shelter and improve their schools and orphanages, all while sharing some fun, laughter and stories. The primary community service would be organized by IRIS (Iowa Resource for International Service), through their offices in Des Moines, Iowa, and their Tanzanian headquarters in the town of Moshi. In addition, the STEMM orphanage, located between Arusha and Moshi and managed by Dr. Steve Meyer, offered a unique chance for the service efforts as this was a new facility that opened during the Kili Bowl event. Another monumental feat, accomplished through extraordinary will and commitment by a rare individual and his team.

In addition to the football game and community service, everybody on the trip would also have a chance to enjoy at least one day on safari in Tarangiri National Park. Then, for those willing and able, the trip would culminate in a climb to the summit of Mt. Kilimanjaro, at 19,341 feet, the rooftop of Africa! Alternatively, for those who chose not to do the summit climb, there was the option of a six-day safari to Lake Manyara, Tarangiri, Ngorongoro Crater, and the Serengeti. All in all, it would be a seventeen-day trip for Drake and sixteen days for CONADEIP. Planning the entire adventure would take about a year and a half.

Everyone in business, actually in every walk of life, at some time has to put a team together in order to accomplish a goal.

From a coach's standpoint, every year a group of young men or women come to the coach and say, "We want to play, we want to be a part of your team." This happens for every youth, high school, college, and professional coach. So the first thing every coach has to do is take the raw components, the athletes, analyze their strengths and weaknesses, and organize the team so that it might perform to its highest level, together.

The same thing happens with every manager in a business. This person in power will have people at all different levels who somehow function together to accomplish the goals that are set. The role of the leader is to put each person in their own best role to achieve the objectives of the organization.

For the Kili Bowl, by autumn 2010 I had the core members of Team Drake and Team Mexico thoroughly involved and moving ahead in their respective areas. Now it was my turn to create another extremely critical team—"Team Tanzania!" I began by meeting, getting to know, and gaining the "buy in" and commitment from a team of individuals in Tanzania who would help me with the myriad of elements needed for the group who would undertake this trip.

This "team" eventually included sincerely dedicated people, each of whom quickly grasped the depth of this dream, and worked seamlessly to make it a reality. Team Tanzania included all of the guides and porters on the Kilimanjaro climb, the workers at the various orphanages and schools, the men and women who helped get the stadium ready to play, our practice facility owners and staff, the hotels' staffs, the drivers, our ground tour operator and his staff, the national tourist board and staff, a vast array of key political leaders who would end up making the event possible, media, and many others who were simply fascinated by the project and joined in to help, adding their own specific expertise.

My list of key contacts in Tanzania is extremely long, but each and every person played a vital role, not only in helping the event to proceed properly, but in producing an experience that would be impactful for all involved, and never forgotten. After months of planning, including three scouting trips to Tanzania, each of the team members listed at the end of this chapter proved to be a critical member of Team Tanzania. And what a powerful team it was!

As I set out to take my first scouting trip to Tanzania, my "team" in this faraway land consisted of Frank Mella, the managing director of what ended up being our primary tour operator Kilele Savane, Ltd. I was introduced to him through email by Sandy Hatfield Clubb, Drake Director of Athletics. Frank, a thirty-three-year-old man, grew up on the slopes of Mt. Kilimanjaro in Marangu Village. After finishing primary school at the age of fifteen, he became a porter on Kili while waiting to be admitted into secondary school. Unfortunately, he was not one of those chosen for the more cost-effective government secondary school, and private schooling was too expensive for his parents. So Frank continued to work on the mountain, hoping to be able to pay for private schooling himself someday. He later enrolled in the mountain guide training courses and became a guide while attending classes. After completing secondary school, Frank worked as a guide for two more years before attending college in Nairobi for three years where he studied Tourism Business Management courses. Upon graduation, he worked in the tourism industry as a Mountain Coordinator and Operations Manager for five years before deciding to establish his own company, Kilele Savane, Ltd., in 2008.

Frank first met Sandy and her father on one of his very first climbs as a porter, and made an instant impression on his clients. Little could he have known what that impression would lead to some fifteen years later. Sandy had told me that Frank was a young man with his own small business who was honest, highly motivated, grew up on the mountain and could do virtually any She assured me that he could set up the entire ground operations for us.

Being a small businessman myself, I am always drawn to others working hard to make it the same way. There are numerous outfitters in Tanzania and East Africa, as the safari and mountain climbing market has continued to expand in recent years due to the wondrous natural beauty of the country. However, with Sandy's recommendation, I felt very comfortable working with Frank and his people. As it turned out, I could not have found a better ally. He ended up being my partner throughout the event, as well as during all of my scouting trips beforehand, and remains a close friend, though far away geographically.

On September 25, 2010, as I prepared for my first nine-day scouting trip to Tanzania, I couldn't help but think about my father, Carl

Steenberge. He worked as a financial manager for the GE Locomotive Division in Erie, Pennsylvania, achieving a management level rarely, if ever, reached by a man without a college degree. He did so through his hard work and honesty. Throughout his career as I was growing up he would often travel to far off lands, bringing back curious stories and fascinating souvenirs. I remembered when I was in eighth grade his returning from a trip to South Africa, and from his suitcase he took out a small wooden camel with a soft leather seat. I can still vividly remember the aroma of the soft leather, so intense and so uniquely different from anything I had ever smelt. During my childhood I was always intrigued by his travel stories, so I guess he sparked my interest in international travel.

For a long time as a young man I had dreamed of going to Africa, but after my first thirteen-month adventure wandering around Latin America at twenty-six, Africa sort of got pushed to the back burner. Now I had my first chance to step foot in Africa and it was exhilarating.

I am not a huge research person, just not my style. On most international scouting trips, I order some maps, get a basic understanding of where I am going, and then learn on the fly. No preconceived ideas. Little worry about what problems I might encounter. I just go, meet folks, tell them what my dream is, and get done what I need to do.

Tanzania, however, was so foreign to me that I tried to read everything I could about my upcoming destination, as my busy life allowed. My wife, Janet, also decided to travel with me on this scouting trip. We had both realized years ago that I was not that much fun to be with during the events I produce. I generally become completely preoccupied with running the tour and taking care of everyone. But the scouting trips are different—challenging, interesting, slower paced, and often rather wild due to the uncertainties. She loves nature and wildlife and adventure, and wasn't about to miss this opportunity to go to Tanzania, experience a safari, see all of the wild animals, and meet the local people.

I had arranged for Frank Mella to meet us at the Kilimanjaro Airport when we landed. Having never been to Africa, I must admit it was strange to fly over entirely unlit lands for hours from Amsterdam, and then touch down in what seemed to be the only lit area for miles around. Of course, the pilots could see the runway lights as we landed. The rest of us just had to believe.

It was here that I met Frank for the first time. He is a lean, athletic Tanzanian in his mid-thirties, who greeted us with a huge smile and a firm handshake. We immediately loaded into his Land Rover and drove to our hotel in Moshi where we would spend the first few nights of our trip. I was instantly impressed by Frank's friendliness, professionalism, and his easygoing nature. I sensed that we would get along well, just as Sandy had told me.

My main goals for this trip to Tanzania were to find a stadium for the game, meet the folks from IRIS who were located in Moshi, experience my first safari, and to meet as many key leaders as I could who would help make the event possible. Most of the political action and corporate business leaders were located in the capital, Dar Es Salaam, so a side trip there was also a must.

Our first day was spent in Moshi, which was really more like a big village, located about thirty minutes east of Kilimanjaro Airport-JRO. I had been told by Del Christensen of IRIS about a small college football stadium there belonging to the local university which he felt would work fine for our game 8 months later. Del had given me a contact name, so Frank and I headed over to check out the stadium. We drove up to this third world looking university, appearing very much like many I had seen in Latin America. There were a number of single-story whitewashed buildings inside a gated entrance where we had to show our ID to be permitted onto campus. There were students, casually dressed, walking here and there between classes. I immediately noticed the openness of the campus. This open-air style of architecture seemed to be prevalent in Tanzania, which only makes sense due to the climate.

We met with the lady in charge of the campus facilities and she directed us to the stadium, telling us the stadium manager would meet us there. The outside of the stadium caught my attention first, a simple wall of yellow cinder blocks. The facility itself was tin-roofed on one side with bleacher seating, while the other side to the north was open without any seats. On the perimeter northern wall, there was a painting of a Kilimanjaro beer commercial which seemed to be omnipresent. In all of the cities, towns, and villages that we visited, mobile phone and beer advertising covered the walls of countless buildings. The Kili beer commercial really struck me, It simply had an outline of Mount Kilimanjaro in the background, snowcapped, with a picture of a bottle of beer and words in the foreground saying, "It's Kili Time! Make the Most of it."

To me it was the perfect ad campaign, and spoke clearly to me, as I was here to plan a historical sporting event in Africa. Surely a key part of my plan was to "make the most of it," and to share that mantra with the young men who would come to Africa. Across the dirt alley from the stadium there were a number of small business vendors, located in what we would use in the United States as temporary sheds perhaps for a weekend festival, but these were their permanent operations. The first structure was a mobile home where a large lady was offering soda, candies, and bread. The next was a shoe store, situated alongside a leather shop, a beauty shop, and about ten or fifteen others. I couldn't help but wonder who actually shopped there?

While Janet and I were taking in the sights and sounds and talking with Frank, we noticed that everybody else was staring at us with great curiosity as we were obviously *wageni* (foreigners).

We headed inside the stadium through the heavy metal door and down the steps to the field, where the effects of the dry season were all too apparent. The entire place looked pretty run down and unkempt with about ten rows of cement bleachers underneath the large metal roof. The field was surrounded by a cinder track that looked as though it hadn't been run on in years, with tufts of grass and weeds growing intermittently.

To the north was a large cloudbank towering over an otherwise clear sky. This, I was told, was hiding Mt. Kilimanjaro. "She is being shy today," Frank told us. We found this to be a very common response when one talked about Kilimanjaro being under cloud cover. As it turned out, this was the normal appearance of Kili. Only on one day, on one scouting trip, was I able to catch a glimpse of the great mountain as the clouds receded. I worried and wondered aloud if I and our future visitors would ever see the summit of Kilimanjaro?

I proceeded to walk around the field, with 'field' being a generous term, as I noticed only about 20 percent of it had any grass coverage, and what was alive was brown and in patches spread out around the field. I looked at the grounds keeper who had been showing us around with a great sense of pride and inquired, "Wow, it's a nice big stadium, with a beautiful view of Mt. Kilimanjaro, but I'm just wondering, is the field always this barren?"

"It's the dry season right now…when is your game?" asked the groundskeeper.

"May," I replied.

"That is good, the grass will be much better then. It will be just after the rainy season."

I thought, all right, that makes sense, but it was still a bit disconcerting. I could not bring college football teams halfway around the world, produce the first American football game ever on the African continent, and play on dirt. The coaches and players would understand many aspects and realities of playing in Tanzania, but we could not play on dirt!

We measured the grounds of the mostly dirt soccer field, it was 140 yards long by 80 yards wide, plenty large enough for an American football field. There were a couple of cement pads at either end of the field next to the track, probably used for basketball. On either side of the cement pads I saw some broken-down metal structures that looked like they could have been scoreboards at some point, though now they just looked like rusted metal frames. The whole stadium looked pretty dirty as it obviously hadn't been cleaned in years, if ever. We continued to walk into the "restrooms" at either end of the grandstand. They were both covered by a metal roof, but only one had a functioning door. Inside were squat toilets, essentially a porcelain hole in the ground. These toilets were not uncommon to countries in Africa, Asia, and even much of Europe, but for unseasoned American travelers, they were a rather unusual concept. Looking at these conditions, I tried to imagine the students' parents, university presidents, local politicians, and any of the important figures we hoped would attend the games having to use these facilities.

The only thing I could say at that point was, "Okay, we can make this work." But I wondered. I started to talk to Frank about perhaps bringing in tents for the teams to use as dressing rooms since there weren't any. We also talked about the use of portable toilets and putting them under a tent for the teams and fans. All of this seemed feasible, it just wasn't a very welcoming sight right now. My first day in Tanzania, my first facility to visit, and this was really not encouraging.

Next we headed around town to look at a range of hotels. We visited some of the small hotels which were nice, and clean, and one larger one that would be suitable. They were all a little outdated with well-used furniture but, I figured, we were in Africa so everybody would understand.

My plan at this point was to set up the teams in the various hotels around town in Moshi, play the game at the local university stadium, and stay there to conduct the service projects as this was the base of operations for IRIS.

The next day Janet and I met with Grace Foya, the director of the IRIS program in Tanzania and her assistant director, Mary Minja. In an instant, after meeting these two women we felt a sense of calm and peacefulness. They were absolutely amazing women whose hearts you could sense were directing their work for the right reasons. It was also great to see that all of the kids seemed to know the two women well and loved them completely. Janet enjoyed spending the entire day with the ladies and the children at the orphanage while I headed back to the university to discuss matters about the stadium and inquire about possible temporary improvements, and contracts for use of the facility.

The facilities manager said they would get the place cleaned up and that, yes, there would be more grass come game day in May (as long as it rained.) That evening we met with a contact of Frank's, Wilfred Onyoni, who was an event organizer in Moshi and would become my key contact there.

Our work and time in Moshi completed, Frank, Janet, and I headed off to Dar Es Salaam. The flight was only an hour and a half, and the view was gorgeous and engrossing with every shade of green below, and plenty of twisted waterways carving their way through the foliage. Dar Es Salaam is southeast of Arusha, right on the Indian Ocean. Upon landing in "Dar," we walked off the twin-engine jet plane and were instantly engulfed in the humidity and heat of this tropical city.

We had been spoiled in Moshi due to the elevation and temperate climate there, where even in September the weather was surprisingly comfortable. During the daytime it was sunny and temperatures reached the mid-eighties, while the evenings would gently cool off. A lot of this is due to the location of Mt. Kilimanjaro just to the north. We came to realize that because of the sheer size of Kili the mountain creates its own weather system and patterns. Strong winds coming off the oceans toward the mountain gathered moisture, eventually colliding with the large mountain slopes where the winds are pushed upward. The fall in temperature and atmospheric pressure lead to precipitation such as snow or rain on the top of the mountain, as well as in the valleys below to the south, where Moshi lay.

Dar Es Salaam, on the other hand, felt like I was back in the hot tropics of Panama City, or Tokyo. Not my favorite climate. With Frank's help, we made our way through the busy, open airport and grabbed a cab into town. Swahili is the native language spoken among the locals, sounding much like Spanish actually, which I am fortunate to speak and understand rather well. English though is also spoken by many people, especially those educated or in the service industry.

Like in most major cities in developing countries the driving was simply wild, and I was certainly happier to be in the hands of a seasoned driver than to have to manage on my own, especially since the driver operated from the right (or wrong) side of the vehicle and drove on the left side of the road. We made it to our nicely appointed hotel on the coast, having somehow woven our way through the masses and myriad of streets.

I promptly started calling around to confirm our meetings, utilizing the Tanzanian mobile phone I had purchased for $20, with minutes costing just pennies. I didn't dare turn on my American Blackberry which would cost me about $4 per minute, from the moment someone started dialing my number, or me calling them. No thanks!

One of the key reasons for my visit to Dar Es Salaam was to meet with members of the Tanzania Tourist Bureau (TTB) to tell them about our upcoming plans and try to elicit their support in promoting the event. The plan was to stage a press conference at noon, which, I had understood, was being set up through Frank and some of the people with whom I had communicated at the TTB before leaving Texas. But when I called to inquire about it on our first day in Moshi, nothing had been arranged. Now that I was in Dar Es Salaam a couple days later and two hours before it was supposed to occur, still nothing had been finalized. Frank then began to call people at the TTB. At this point I started to get a bit concerned, wondering why I had come all this way to Dar for something that might not occur. I could hear the conversations but was only able to get bits and pieces as they would go back and forth between English and Swahili. Frank told me they were happy to prepare a press conference and would call the media at this time, two hours before it was scheduled! Having produced numerous events in Latin America, as well as countries throughout Europe and Asia, I realized that other cultures operated differently from ours and tried to relax, and believe.

After checking into our rooms, Frank and I decided to take the fifteen-minute walk over to the TTB office. I had on my light wool sport coat, khaki pants and boots, shirt and tie, prepared for a meeting, but by the time we arrived at the building I was drenched with sweat from the tropical heat and moisture. Inside the building lobby there was very little light. It was almost as hot as outside and there were many people understandably wearing short sleeve shirts. We took the elevator up, got off and went straight to the room where we were told the press conference was to be held. Frank and I took a seat and waited about ten minutes or so until the managing director, Mr. A. C. Macha, arrived. He was an engaging, large, and robust man, befitting his role as the country's primary tourism promoter.

One of the key issues I knew I would come across in arranging a football game in Africa was that most people I met with had absolutely zero knowledge of American football. Some had seen it on television or movies, and a few of the better-traveled had heard a bit more about it, but it was still a very foreign concept to them. I would have to begin by explaining the basics of the game to everybody I met on my scouting trips, from the political leaders to the people in industry and trade, to the hotel operators and media.

They often likened it to rugby since it was a more familiar sport to them. Rugby was first introduced to East Africa by the white settlers in the mid-1900s and had since grown in popularity. One of the most important, and entertaining things I did to help explain football on a more basic level and to gain interest everywhere I went on my trips was to carry with me a blue Drake University helmet and a football. They turned out to be ideal conversation points. I showed everybody the helmet, and welcomed them to put it on, which most everybody was eager to do. Children were always the most excited. I demonstrated the Heisman pose for them, something the doorman at the Sea Cliff Hotel had the most fun replicating. I would then be able to capture some wonderful photos. I also brought my laptop with me to show video clips of other Global Football tours in Europe and Central America. This easily allowed everyone to see what the game looked like, how it was played, and, most importantly, why they should be interested in helping me bring it to Tanzania.

After meeting with Mr. Macha, having fun showing him the props and posing for the photos, I inquired about the press conference. He told me the media had been called. I was still a little apprehensive as to whether or not this would happen. But then, about fifteen minutes later, the room filled with three television cameras and ten reporters with microphones.

I sat there in complete amazement that all of these people showed up on the spur of the moment. I proceeded to tell the story about American football and plans for the first-ever Global Kilimanjaro Bowl. They were clearly intrigued and asked basic questions. I was thrilled with how the press conference went, especially after my skepticism earlier in the day.

We spent the rest of the day in the vibrant city known simply as "Dar." I kept trying to get hold of Lazaro Nyalandu to formally meet him, knowing that he would be a critical contact in Tanzania, having been introduced via email by Dr. Steve Meyer. However, as the Deputy

Minister of Industry and Trade, he was often called out of the country at a moment's notice. While he was instrumental in arranging some of my key contacts for this first trip, due to his extremely busy schedule he proved to be a very difficult person to reach, and I never did get to meet him on this scouting trip.

That mid-afternoon we did arrange to sit down with the most charming and influential man, Col. Iddi Kipingu, retired, and Minister of Sport for Tanzania. Colonel Kipingu was a slight, spry man. I figured him to be in his sixties, but it was hard to tell. He was another casual, easy-to-smile character who was instantly enthralled with my story of bringing American football to his country. He was a high school principal, his day job, and totally committed to encouraging youngsters to play sports of any type. The idea of a new sport coming to Tanzania was most interesting to him. Also, as South Africa had just hosted the World Cup of Soccer (football as it is called in most the world), he thought it most fascinating that Tanzania could host the first American football game! We became instant friends. His assistance, while often quietly behind the scenes, was powerful leading up to and including the actual event.

Evening rolled around and the cool on-shore breezes set in, making the setting magical to sit out on the veranda of the restaurant and enjoy a comfortable meal. Janet, Frank, and I decided to meet up with one of Frank's cousins, of which there seemed to be many. This cousin, Mr. Gaudence Tamu, was the Chief Executive Officer at Swissport Tanzania Ltd. His company managed the baggage handling at the international airports. While we discussed our teams coming over in May with him, he explained to me that it would be very difficult for my football teams to lose their baggage on their way over to Tanzania. He went on to explain that flights coming from Amsterdam went directly to Kilimanjaro Airport in Arusha, then on to Dar Es Salaam, and back through Arusha the next day on their way back to Amsterdam. Therefore, the chance of luggage getting lost between Amsterdam and Arusha was nearly zero, but even if luggage were left on the plane and made its way to Dar Es Salaam, it would be right back to Arusha the next day. His professionalism and knowledge of the system helped put me at ease about this risk as I knew we would be in good hands. I had been concerned, realizing that the players would practice just twice before the game, which would take place only three days after landing. The odd times we have had delayed or lost equipment on tours to other countries we had been able to reach out to local teams to borrow a helmet, shoulder pads, or whatever. Clearly this would not be possible in Tanzania.

After just one night and day in Dar Es Salaam we were off to the part of the trip both Janet and I had anticipated the most, the safari, which, of course, Frank had arranged for us. From Dar, we flew north in a small, twenty-four-passenger twin-engine airplane that cruised only about eight thousand feet or so above the ground. Our low altitude allowed us spectacular views as we headed back toward the Arusha airport, just outside of the city that serves as the hub of northern Tanzania. I had not been in a small plane in years and felt a bit nervous with every bump and hitch that we took. The pilot, a British man I believe, seemed very bright and shared his knowledge about all the sights we were flying over, but, still a bit nervous, all I could think about was that there was no such thing as OSHA or FAA in Tanzania.

After landing we were told to wait for the next hour and a half for our bush plane to arrive and take us to the Serengeti, where we would begin our four-day safari. In the meantime, we wandered around the "lobby" of the airport. Essentially, the lobby was a large metal-roofed building with intermittent sides, mostly open air spaces, a couple of shops, and seating.

It also boasted one of the best signs I had ever seen. The simple rectangular posting had an extensive list of items that could not be taken on the airplane, including things like rifles, explosives, machetes, bows and arrows, and even blow darts! Glad I had left my blow dart at home. With very little direction as to which plane was ours among the dozens that came and went on the asphalt apron, we finally found our way to our little eightseater in which there were four passengers—two others, Janet, and me.

Shortly into our trip we began to make an unexpected (for us) landing next to a small village. As I was quickly learning, each day in

Tanzania would bring a series of unexpected, but marvelous events. Just adjust, with poise, I kept reminding myself. As we began to land I noticed we were flying west, directly toward a vertical thousand-foot high escarpment. I found out later that this wall is part of the Great Rift Valley which is approximately a six-thousand-mile long trough that runs from northern Syria through Tanzania south to central Mozambique. The East African Rift System (EARS) is an area where the earth's tectonic plates are moving apart, creating a valley over the new plates underneath. Without ever really descending, we landed on a small dirt runway next to the village. We only stopped long enough to pick up two more passengers. Taking off was a bit disconcerting as the airplane gained speed, but remained at the same elevation while the cliff just dropped below us.

Soon we flew over Lake Manyara, one of Tanzania's National Parks praised by Ernest Hemingway as "the loveliest I had seen in Africa." We then made our way over a huge caldera, Ngorongoro Crater, and onto the Serengeti where we caught our first glimpse of African wildlife below. This is what I had come to see. Below was a myriad of trails carved through the dry land, the etched stories of annual migrations and daily forays in search of food and water. With its scrub brush and arid appearance, the landscape reminded me somewhat of Bolivia's Altiplano which I had visited some thirty-five years earlier.

We descended gently and landed in the heart of the Serengeti where we planned to meet David, a coworker of Frank's and our safari guide. David is a slender man, about 6 feet 3 inches tall with long limbs and a gentle face. We shook hands. He loaded our bags into the Land Rover and headed over to fill out some paperwork before leaving the airport grounds. Everywhere one went in Tanzania it seemed there was always a great deal of government paperwork to complete and submit. Similar to Latin America, I often found myself wondering where all those completed paper forms end up. Just curious if anyone ever sees them again, or if there is some gigantic government building in each country, possibly an airplane hangar, keeping them all secure?

As we waited for David we looked around at the dirt runway and saw a small medical plane, parked. It seemed pretty quiet until all of a sudden a medical helicopter emerged over the tree line and started to land. The chopper appeared to have two people strapped to the skids of the helicopter in stretchers. The attending medical personnel worked frantically to get the injured parties off the helicopter and onto the waiting airplane. Our curiosity began to run wild. By then David had come back to the vehicle, papers in hand, and while driving off we asked him,"What was that all about?"

"A safari air balloon went down while flying over the Serengeti. I understand that a couple of people were killed while the people you saw survived but were badly injured."

Wow, we thought as we headed out with David, that is a little too much excitement for our first few minutes on safari.

The Land Rover was perfect, ideally constructed for such rugged work with seats for six, providing plenty of room for the three of us. It also had a roof that popped up, allowing us to stand next to the seats and gaze out at the wildlife without obstruction while still in the comfort and safety of our vehicle.

Within the first thirty minutes of being in the Serengeti, we had virtually seen all the animals I had ever expected to see— multitudes of zebras, giraffes, and elephants of all ages and sizes wandering here and there, tearing through vegetation as they went. We saw all sorts of antelope, from the precious tiny dik dik to the gracefully swift gazelle. We also viewed some of Africa's not so pretty creatures like the hyena and warthog, or "Pumba," which seemed to be everywhere. Janet and I were like kids in a candy shop fascinated by the diversity of wildlife and trying as hard as we could to take everything in.

I imagined that David, who lived this daily, could easily have gotten bored seeing the same creatures day in and day out, but he was highly animated and engaging, taking great care to point out every creature he could. All the while, sharing his encyclopedialike knowledge about the habitat, mating, gestation period, diet, life cycles, predators and any other interesting facts that went along with the different species we encountered. He kept three zipper-closed, canvas-covered guidebooks handy on the dashboard that seemed to be there more for our benefit. Inside these books were answers to everything, but rarely did he have to reference them, as he knew the Serengeti well.

En route we stopped by a hippopotamus pool, which was like nothing I had ever imagined. I always thought of hippos as hefty, lazy, rather charming creatures, spending their days peacefully immersed in lazy rivers. Near this particular hippo pool was an overlook where David allowed us to get out of the car to get a better view. The area was about fifty yards by thirty yards where the river widened slightly into a stagnant, greenish-grey pool of water. Within that space, about 90 percent of the surface water area was occupied by the bulbous bodies of hippos. They were everywhere, piled up, young and old, male and female, restless due to their tight confines, constantly jostling for position. They sunk under water for brief lengths of time, holding their breath, then rising up with rounded ears and nostrils popping out before their slick, wide-berth backs. It was fascinating to see them all living, eating, breathing, and pooping, something they seemed to do quite often. They swished their little tails around like small propellers to spread out the green oozing from their rear ends. David simply told us "he is cleaning his bottom." Their large, round eyeballs and wide yawns provided a captivating scene. Peering at the bacteria-infested pool with massive mammals seemingly enjoying themselves, I turned to David and asked, "What would happen if I jumped into the pool with them?"

He paused, and with a short laugh just said, "You would die."

During the safari we encountered many other groups, similar to ours, traveling in Land Rovers of all shapes and sizes. Most were filled up with tourists bearing long-lens cameras and classic safari garb. With only two of us clients in a six-passenger vehicle, we were being nicely spoiled. The drivers all knew one another and stopped to talk as they passed, sharing stories and locations of animals. I instantly learned just how gregarious and friendly the Tanzanians are. All day David would weave in and out of different dirt roads, avoiding some of the potholes, pointing out sights and sounds while somehow not getting lost.

Throughout the trip I checked out a number of prospective lodges for the safari that we might use during the event, as that was our primary reason for being here. Our first night we stayed in a lodge tucked away in little foothills and made up entirely of tents, and nicely appointed semipermanent structures. There was a cement floor and knee wall, canopy bed, dressers, soft chairs, couches, closet, clean bathroom with shower, just about all any hotel room might offer. Our particular tent/room was about seventy- five yards from the main tent which held the large lobby, dining room, bar, and gift shop. We checked in with a young man who helped us to haul our bags to our tent and told us to call him on the phone when we were ready for dinner so he could come get us. We hated to put him through any trouble and told him it would be easy for us just to walk there. He explained to us that this would not be safe as there were wild animals roaming around at night and this wasn't exactly a secure confine. It was a stark reminder of where we, in fact, were. Out of the ten lodging tents, ours was the furthest from the main lobby, located on the edge of the grounds which sloped down into a little wooded area.

Thirty feet away from our tent door was a big rounded rock that stood about one hundred feet high and was a few hundred feet in diameter. I thought, *What a great place that would be to watch the sunrise or sunset.* After a great meal and night's sleep, I awoke to the sounds of the African wilderness just as dawn began to appear. Janet was still sleeping, but I had a hard time going back to sleep so I headed outside to look for animals and enjoy the total quietude. Putting on my light jacket, I headed out to the massive rock and scuttled up the side to the top, looked out over the expanse of the savannah. I had been in Moshi, in Dar Es Salaam, and on the airplanes, but now I was experiencing Africa, personally. As I was taking in the scenery and looking for animals that appeared to be in hiding, the young man who helped us the night before walked up to our tent to retrieve us for breakfast. I started down the rock toward him.

"Patrick, why are you here alone?"

"I woke up early and wanted to see some animals."

"That is not safe, please be more careful."

I thought, *Well, I am glad it was safe this morning.*

We were able to sit and talk while Janet took some pictures and then headed, escorted, to breakfast. David, who always slipped away at night to go sleep elsewhere, I'm guessing some sort of staff housing, came to retrieve us for our second day of safari. On the road out of the Serengeti we came across our first lion, as well as a spotted leopard lying down on the lowest limb of a distant tree. David had the keenest eyes of any man I have known, spotting the most concealed creatures off in the distance and pointing them out. Along the way we made lists of animals we saw and tried hard to learn their names in Swahili. Pumbaa was easy. The pronunciations being just like Spanish enabled me to read the names from David's books, or when he would spell it and I would write it down.

Antelope- *Swala*
Baboon- *Nyani*
Black Monkey- *Kima*
Cheetah- *Duma*
Crocodile- *Mamba*
Dikdik- *Funo*
Egyptian Goose- *Mmisri bata bakini*
Elephant- *Tembo*
Gazelle- *Swala*
Giraffe- *Twiga*
Grant's Gazelle- *Swala Granti*
Hippopotamus- *Kiboko*
Hyena- Fisi
Impala- *Swala Pala*

Jackal- *Bweha*
Leopard- *Chut*
Lion- *Simba*
Mongoose- *Nguchiro*
Monkey- *Kima*
Ostrich- *Mbuni*
Rhinoceros- *Kifaru*
Safari ants- *Siafu*
Thompson's Gazelle- *Swala Tomi*
Vervet Monkey- *Tumbili/Tumbiri*
Warthog- *Ngiri*
Water Buffalo- *Nyati*
Wildebeest- *Nyumbu*
Zebra- *Punda Milia*

While making our way across a wide open dusty plain for a little over an hour, we came across our first groups of Maasai. Off in the distance were their round huts encircled by barriers of brush, briar, and bushes to keep their livestock in and the wild animals out of the compound at night. The scene appeared just as I imagined it had been for centuries. Scattered across the open expanse were small herds of gaunt cattle, with young boys, about five to ten years of age, holding sticks and spears tending to them. They stood out in the distance with their black and red clothing whipping in the wind, wearing sandals made of rubber tires. It was clear to me that this was life as it has always been in the Serengeti.

Finally, we climbed a switch-backed hillside, gained elevation from the level of the Serengeti and came to a forested area where our lodge for the night was located. This classic looking African lodge was impressive, built with huge boulders and stones with dark wood lining the inside. Our room had an open rock porch off the back with an impressive view looking down over the Ngorongoro crater, which would turn out to be my favorite nature park of the trip. This amazing conservation area and World Heritage Site was actually a massive volcanic caldera. The crater was formed roughly two or three million years ago when a volcano exploded and collapsed in on itself. About two thousand feet deep, its floor covers some one hundred square miles. The crater serves as a natural enclosure for the plethora of animals that roam the expansive area.

I sat outside on the porch gazing out at the crater below, contemplating how long this crater had been there and wondered just how many animals thrived down there. All of a sudden I heard a loud rustling noise in the brush, got up from my chair and looked through the three foot round hole in the rocks to investigate. To my surprise, not ten feet away was an elephant crashing away through the tall bamboo thickets. It all happened so fast that it was somewhat of an apparition; I sat back wondering if what I thought I had seen was truly real.

The next day we headed out for our safari through Ngorongoro crater, which I discovered to be even more impressive than the Serengeti in terms of sheer numbers of animals. As we descended the windy dirt road towards the crater base I asked David if we would see a lion that day, to which he casually replied with a twinkle in his eye, "If we are lucky."

Ngorongoro had a bit more tourist traffic, but it didn't seem to affect the teeming herds of wildebeest. At one point we stopped to view a small group of them being chased by a lean, stealthy wild cat. As we watched the drama play out, it was as if we were viewing a National Geographic film.

Further down the path, about a hundred yards off, there had been a kill. We watched as two female lions were devouring what looked to be a wildebeest, recently killed. As they were trying to patiently enjoy their meal, half a dozen jackals hung around the perimeter taunting the lions, working to distract them and get their fair share of the meal. We stopped abruptly, where about ten feet from the roadside there lounged three large male lions, one older with a large mane and two younger ones. I took photos while they seemed unconcerned, simply enjoying their post-meal siesta, posing for us, it appeared, where we could almost reach out and touch them! David informed us that while the females are in charge of the hunting, the males get first dibs on the food and when they are full, the females get to finish off what is left of their kill. We sat there for about forty-five minutes, maybe longer, with cameras in hand trying our hardest to capture a moment that we would probably never relive.

A little further along, we caught a whiff of the worst smell I had ever experienced, emanating from an injured hyena. The poor guy had somehow been wounded as was evident by the nasty, bloody back end. I decided soon after that hyenas would not be my animal of choice to hang out with.

We continued along throughout the morning with wild animals of every shape and size and color and species visible in all directions, and then stopped at a picnic area in the crater near a sizable lake. There were probably thirty vehicles with tourists eating at a number of picnic tables. We sat at our table and asked David why this seemed to be a safe area where animals tended to stay away from, as there were so many tourists out of their vehicles. Nowhere else were we permitted outside on foot. Before he could respond, we heard yelping and loud talking as everybody quickly started to pack back into their vehicles. We decided to follow suit, when all of a sudden we noticed two adult lions ambling down the hillside toward the parking lot. Once there, they weaved their way up and down the parking lot between the vehicles. They looked fairly tame and used to humans, though David promptly reminded us that all that would change if we stepped out of the vehicle onto their turf. We sat for at least fifteen minutes watching the lions examining the area, when they decided to head over toward the cement beach-house-looking restroom facility. As the one lion decided to lie down and sunbathe right in front of the ladies bathroom door, I couldn't help but wonder, What if somebody was still in there? We didn't stay to find out. So much for a safe spot to picnic.

That afternoon we headed out of Ngorongoro toward Arusha and through Arusha National Park. This day was simply overwhelming! Still excited by every animal we saw, as we rocked along yet another dusty road I noticed a tiny baboon in a rivulet, near the small Momella Lake. It seemed to be washing its hands in the water, sipping at times and just enjoying the peaceful setting. I wondered where the rest of his family was, as baboons, I had learned from David, always seemed to travel in family packs often numbering in the dozens. Soon we were on the flatland, with one hundred yards of tall, tufted grass between us, and the lakefront shore where ducks, flamingos, egrets and other waterfowl hung out.

Alongside the waterfront some 60 yards away I noticed a group of baboons of various sizes walking left to right in single file. At first I didn't think much of it as baboons, oddly enough, had become commonplace for us during our short visit. But wait, the fourth in line of seven was a small white animal, at a distance, appearing possibly to be a large bird, or small cat, or even…a white baboon? I quickly asked David to stop and pointed out to him the seemingly white baboon. David peered out but couldn't see the wandering troupe due to his lower placement in the driver's seat. He began to back up for a better view. After about thirty yards, he stopped on a slight hill and saw it…yes…it was an albino baboon, he told us. And in fact, he had never seen one in his thirty years of living in Africa and guiding tours. I atattempted a few photos on my simple digital camera, wishing at that moment that I had one of those long lens units most people on safari carry. It was truly amazing to catch such a rare glimpse of African wildlife and only helped reemphasize how blessed we were to be on this life-enhancing journey.

We made our drive all the way back to Arusha that night. It was my first experience with being in a car at night in Tanzania, which I now understand was one of the most dangerous things to do there, maybe even more dangerous than hopping into a hippo pool or getting out of the Range Rover on safari. On the road into Arusha, which of course had no street lights, it seemed like every one hundred yards or so there was a person walking with no thought of wearing brightly colored clothing for us to see to avoid hitting them. There were cows, horses, mules, all types of domestic animals lining the roads. There were people on bicycles, sometimes one person, sometimes two, sometimes going against traffic and sometimes with traffic. There seemed to be no order or flow to anything on this two lane stretch of grey pavement. Traffic moved quickly, veering left and right to avoid the many obstacles. Somehow it worked!

One of the most memorable signs I saw as we came into town was on the back of a large passenger bus as it chugged by us and in big letters proclaimed, "In We God Trust." Sometimes translation is difficult.

As we arrived on the outskirts of Arusha, David decided the traffic was just too horrible on the one main road into town so he decided to go safari style, taking the back roads to avoid traffic. The city back streets were worse than those on safari, which was hard to believe, as we bobbed and weaved around the massive holes in the road. Amazingly, we reached the hotel without striking anything too large along the way. The hotel had a small boutique style to it and was owned by a Swiss friend of Frank's, who had his office on the grounds of the hotel. Each small bungalow had one or two rooms in them with a nice canopy bed and sculpted wooden furniture. It was an impeccably clean, magical little place with a swimming pool and lobby room where we enjoyed our dinner.

The following morning before our flight home to the States we were able to meet with Frank and his family. I had corresponded with Frank many times via email preparing for this trip, and during this journey, so I knew him to be focused and professional in his work. But I was not prepared for the personal grace and quiet charm he exuded as I spent time with him. His French wife was lovely, and the children, Nicolas and Sylvia, were full of playfulness and innocence while living in a land of such overt poverty.

David, our guide, was such a kind and humble man who was clearly an observer and educator with a service mentality, possibly even surpassing that of the Japanese. He was so proud to show us his recently purchased plot of land outside Arusha, backed by the towering Mount

Meru, where he intended to build his house, step by step, brick by brick, as he earned and saved money for each segment of its construction.

Wilfred, who was to be our Moshi-man and seemed to know everyone in that town of a hundred thousand (though it appeared much smaller), had an easy smile and sharp mind to enhance his quick wit. Among the officials we met with, Colonel (rtd) Iddi Omari Kibingu, Commissioner of the National Sports Council, was the most impressive to me. It was his ease of manner, eagerness to help and welcoming spirit that I liked best. It also helped that we had similar visions as to the impact the Kili Bowl would have on the youth of Tanzania and the potential for future learning through sport.

Each person we met in the lodges, restaurants and shops happily and sincerely greeted us with cool fresh juice, a quick *jambo* (hello), and then *karibu* (welcome), the most often heard phrase in the language. When leaving, it was always *asante* (thank you). These were not just greetings, but honest, heartfelt verbal embraces.

Being somewhat of a veteran traveler of Europe, Latin America, parts of Asia, and of course America, I try not to preconceive what I am likely to witness and what the people that I encounter will be like. Rather, I just go, enlisting the help of a local person there to assist me and plan out an aggressive itinerary of travel and meetings. My trips are most always workrelated, which allows me to travel often, and these personal travel experiences are a major reason I have chosen my line of work. As I headed back to Texas, I must say I knew that this particular journey would stay with me forever.

My stated mission on this trip was to prepare for the upcoming Global Kilimanjaro Bowl event in May, where American football would be brought to this continent for the first time in history. There was so much packed into this one-week on the ground that my mind was left swimming with visions, memories and words I had sought to learn in Swahili. I was now far better prepared to tell my future travelers about what they would encounter, should they choose to be a part of the teams coming from Drake University and the CONADEIP league teams of Mexico, or join the Fans and Families Tour groups who would come to enjoy, cheer, and experience.

I now knew that we had a uniquely talented team of people in Tanzania who could insure that every aspect of the upcoming tour would be special and life-changing in many ways for those who participated. It was also obvious how much more work there was to be done here.

There was much to be done now, as arranging the next steps began: flights, baggage and transportation, practices, youth clinics, one-day safaris for team members, lodge accommodations, meals, water, local transport, guides, tour coordinators, orphanage visits, service work at numerous children's homes, Kilimanjaro climb, permits and permissions, media coverage and, of course, the game, with all its necessary pomp and circumstance, helping the local people understand and enjoy the contest.

During the rest of my scouting trips and time at home while preparing for the big event, I continued to meet with highly respected Tanzanian individuals, at times completely alter large segments of the itineraries, try to find sponsors who would believe in the value of the Global Kilimanjaro Bowl, and put together a team of individuals-friends, family and colleagues, without whom this event would not have been possible.

View from the Summit

Many have stated more eloquently than me how life is a journey, rather than a destination, and this first week in Africa, in Tanzania, reinforced that so clearly. Each day, each moment, overwhelmed my senses with a bombardment of sights, sounds, smells and tastes I had never before experienced, even though I had previously traveled far and wide. I found each person I encountered to be unique in spirit, with a caring and pleasantness unrivaled in my world. I had come to Tanzania to prepare for a football game and tour, and soon realized that this would be so much more for our football teams, our clients, our friends, and for me.

Heck, I had seen an Albino Baboon!

Team Tanzania

Hotels

- **The Arusha Hotel**
    - Japhet Kithinji—Front Office Manager
    - Catherine Lloyd—Sales and Marketing Manager

- **Kilimanjaro Hotel**
    - Trevor Saldanha—General Manager

- **Moshi Leopard Hotel**
    - Priscus Tarimo—Marketing Director

- **Kibo Palace Hotel**
    - Salahuddin Ahmad—Director
    - Patricia Oisso—Sales and Marketing Officer
    - Charity Githinji—Sales and Marketing Manager

Volunteers

- Dr. Steve Meyer—President/Founder of STEMM
- Del Christensen—Executive Director IRIS
- Grace Foya—Tanzania Director of IRIS
- Mary Minja—Assistant Director at IRIS
- Jeff Hollister—Managing Director, Peace House Africa
- Tyler Satterlund—Volunteer Coordinator, Peace House Africa

Government

- **Embassies**
    - Roberto Quiroz—US Embassy in Tanzania
    - Alfonso Lenhardt—American Ambassador to Tanzania
    - Luis Javier Campuzano—Mexican Ambassador to East Africa

- **Tanzania National Parks Authority (TANAPA):**
  - Allan Kijaze—Acting Director General (one who called me in the men's room at DFW)
  - Johnson Manase—Manager Tourism Services
  - Joseph Kessy—Principal Planner
  - Diocless Emmanuel—Principal Tourism Promotion Officer
  - Pascal Shelutete—Public Relations Manager
  - Lukonge Philip Mhandagani—Board Member of TANAPA

- **Ministry of Information, Culture, and Sports**
  - Dr. Emmanuel Nchimbi—Minister
  - Raphael Hokororo—Assistant Director
  - Clement Mshana—Director of Information Services

- **National Sports Council**
  - Henry Lihaya—Secretary General
  - Colonel Iddi Kipingu (retired)—Director
  - John Chalukulu—Senior Sports Officer

- **Tanzania Tourist Board (TTB)**
  - C. Macha—Managing Director
  - Augustina Makoye—Public Relations Officer II
  - Willy Lyimo—Branch Manager Arusha
  - Devota Mdachi—Ag. Principal Marketing Officer
  - Geofrey Meena—Marketing Manager
  - Geofrey Tengeneza—Principal Public Relations Officer

- **Other Government Employees**
  - Governor Isidore Leka Shirima—Regional Commissioner of Arusha
  - Karen Hoffman—NY with Bradford Group represents Tanzania Tourism
  - Alhaj Kassim Mamboleo—Protocol Officer in Regional Commissioner Office Arusha

- o Ezekiel Maige—Minister of Natural Resources in Tourism
- o Goodluck Ole-Medeye—Deputy Minister of the Ministry of Lands, Housing, and Human Settlements Development
- o Dr. Abdulla Saadalla—Deputy Minister of the East African Corporation
- o Dr. Cyrilir Chami—Tanzania Minister of Industry and Trade
- o Paul Mella—Tanzania Military Intelligence Chief (Frank Mella's Cousin)
- o Wilfred Onyoni—Moshi Events Coordinator
- o Lucas Lifa Ng'hoboko—Assistant Commissioner of Police
- o CCM Chama Cha Mapinduzi—Political party which owns Arusha stadium

Sport (Non-Governmental)
- o Francis John—President, Athletics Tanzania
- o Andre De Beer—Arusha Irie

Television–Independent Television LTD (ITV):
- o Dr. Reginald Mengi—Chairman/Owner
- o Joyce Mhaville—Managing Director (my main contact)
- o Joyce Luhanga—Director of Sales and Marketing
- o Macharia Koigi—Channel Director
- o Frank Mshana—Asst. cameraman

Tanzania Horticulture Association (TAHA)
- o Jacqueline Mkindi—Executive Director
- o Naiga Malilo—Marketing and Information Officer
- o Tjerk Scheltema—Multiflower Ltd and TAHA Board Chairman (met with first for protocol)

Tour Guides
- o Frank Mella—Director of Kileli Savane Ltd.
- o Peter Mato—Tour Guide for Kileli Savane Ltd with CONADEIP team

- o David Awed—Lead Guide for Kilele Savane Ltd.

Publications
- o Lynn Taylor—*PAA Magazine* Editor
- o Dar Life Team—*Dar Life* Magazine

Other
- o Mongollah Segulle—Tanzania Coca-Cola Bonita Bottler
- o Gaudence Tamu—Chief Executive Officer at Swissport Tanzania Ltd.
- o Saifudin Khanbhai—Managing Director of Cultural Heritage Limited

The true lasting memories of travel are not the sights and sounds and smells, but rather the people, each of whom have their uniqueness. If the world is a panorama with a kaleidoscope of colors bringing all things to life, then each person has a distinct color and shade and gradient he or she reflects. Countries and cultures are known more for their "peoples," than for their natural wonders. We travel to experience and to learn and to enjoy. It is those who help and direct us along the way and with whom we share these moments that, in fact, color our lasting impressions.

5

It's Not the X's and O's, It's the Jims and Joes

FOOTBALL—THE GREATEST EXAMPLE OF TEAMWORK THAT EXISTS IN SPORTS, can be translated to any group working together to achieve a goal, whether in business, academics, organizations, politics or family. If a company or organization could work together as does a championship football team, with each player performing his or her role, selflessly committed to success, adjusting as needed to market conditions and opposing forces, then this group would surely succeed. Business and organizational leaders want their staff to emulate winning athletic teams, and with good reason. That is why coaches and players from championship teams are such highly sought-after public speakers. They are leaders and great teammates.

(Left to right) Jennie Phillips, John Roslien, Mike Preston, Patrick Steenberge, Xela Steenberge, and Tim Brockman.

I began playing organized ball at the age of ten, and was quickly exposed to the greatest example of teamwork, football. While I always understood that it was teamwork which would make my team so much better than other more talented squads, it was not until decades later that I truly would comprehend the dynamics of football's teamwork.

The offense makes a plan in the huddle which they must execute within three to four seconds. To win the game, the offense has to be able to execute those brief plays successfully, about sixty to seventy times.

The defense must, at the same time, work together to stop the offensive plays, analyzing and guessing what the offense's plan of action might be and trying to counter it. As the offense, you know that those eleven defensive guys are going to try to stop you but you just aren't quite sure how until each play starts. Will the defense use a 4-3 or 3-4 alignment and are they going to use blitzes or stunts to try and throw you off balance? For each play, both sides must constantly adjust on the fly to what the other is doing, as they work to accomplish their own goals.

In business and most any organization, this also occurs, and was exactly what my "Team Global" had to do during the creation and execution of the Kili Bowl. We had our initial plan of action, but it constantly evolved in response to issues that came our way throughout the planning and production of the plan.

For every event I produce, wherever in the world it is staged, I put together a Team Global, a group of individuals who bring their various skills and talents to the field and help make the event possible and successful. For Tanzania, I was fortunate to invite and rely upon an all-star team of friends and family who have each been a part of my life at some point. As a wonderful result of our work on the Kili Bowl, they are now much closer friends!

If the individuals I was blessed with to help produce the Kili Bowl were aligned in a football model, it would look something like this:

Offense

Let me explain the offensive lineup for our Team Global

Center *Chris Creighton: Drake University Head Coach*

In football, each and every play begins when the center moves the ball off of the ground and into the hands of the quarterback. Depending on the particular play, this can be accomplished in a couple of different styles, but nothing happens until the center moves the ball.

Chris got this entire project moving, making him the Center of Team Global Tanzania. While to some he was seen as the face of the event, he was most often an unsung hero who was satisfied just to do his job for the good of the team. When all is said and done on the football field, the center always plays a pivotal if underrated role. It was the same here.

Guard *J. C. Maya: CONADEIP Head Coach*

The guard must block the defense on both running and passing plays. He has a specified assignment on each play, whereby he initiates movement, but each movement is also a reaction to the defenders who are trying to find and stop the person with the football.

Coach Maya had the challenging, delicate role of selecting an all-star team from the eighteen CONADEIP member teams, and then, with just a few practices, put them on the field in Arusha, Tanzania to face an unknown, quality team—the Drake Bulldogs. Maya did an excellent job of getting his team ready for the game as well as, and more importantly, for the entire scope of the trip. He also was heavily involved in the public service projects and joined his players in summiting Mt. Kilimanjaro.

Guard *Xela Steenberge: Family and Friends Group Coordinator*

The offensive guards' job, while appearing to the unknowing fan to be simple, actually involves many skills. Quickness, strength, agility and adjustment are needed, as they must block/ move the defender in front of them so as to allow the ball carrier to have an open lane in which to run.

Xela had done solid work for me on a few events prior to this one. She was knowledgeable about how my typical events ran and helped to ensure the family and friends were well taken care of throughout the entire trip, allowing me to focus on other aspects of the event. While she was instrumental to me in this event, it also helped her gain valuable contacts in Tanzania for her career. After the completion of the event, she was able to stay for a physical therapy internship at the Arusha Lutheran Medical Center before her final year of undergraduate work at the University of Tampa.

Tackle *Michael Preston: Media Director*

The Offensive Tackle is the key offensive lineman. This is especially true of the left tackle as he defends the quarterback's blind side, where he is most vulnerable. He must also be able to block the largest, fastest defensive player, the defensive end.

Mike is British by birth and moved to the United States in 2002. When I met him in the late nineties, Mike was working with NFL Europe and NFL International. During that time, I was running a Super Bowl event I had created called the NFL Global Junior Championship and worked with Mike on the media side of things. After working for the NFL, he decided to form his own media consulting business. I became one of his clients and have since utilized his talents for all of my events. When we started to work on the Kili Bowl together it turned out that he and the Sports Information Director at Drake, who happened to have been hired there about six months prior to the event, were long time friends. Mike worked diligently with me to promote the Kili Bowl around the world through various media prior to, during and after the event.

Tackle *John Roslien aka 'JR': Game Day Operations, Announcer, DJ, Stadium Preparation and Logistics*

The right tackle has a very similar role to the left tackle in leading the charge against the defense, thereby allowing the quarterback to throw or the running back to carry the ball forward. He is constantly making adjustments instantaneously, keeping his head "on a swivel."

JR's role was broad and varied. He was to set up the game field, announce the game live in-stadium and assist with other tasks as needed. The field preparation alone was a monumental task, working with local people who had never seen an American football field or game in person or on television! One can imagine the scope of work that had to be done when you take into account that this was a grass soccer stadium with a cinder track around it as well as a cement curb. There were no goal posts, lines, announcer's booth, TV booth or sound system when JR began his work. These efforts were likely not noticed by anyone except possibly the coaches and myself, thus allowing others to be the star players.

John is head of the Physical Training Department at Central College Iowa and has been a trusted ally for the past sixteen years. He is the only person other than myself to have worked each of the sixteen Global Football Division III All-Star games in Mexico.

Quarterback *Patrick Steenberge: President of Global Football, Event Producer*

The QB calls the offensive plays, telling each teammate what their role is during the next three to four seconds. In 'football jargon,' these names and signals are communicated in the huddle in just a few seconds. Then the QB is the first to receive the ball at the start of the play, followed by giving the ball to a running back, running it himself, or passing to one of the receivers. While the play given in the huddle provides an outline and strategy, depending on how exactly the defense aligns and adjusts, the QB must also adjust.

In Tanzania, as well as during the preparation time leading up to the event, I was the overseer who called the plays, analyzed the obstacles and resources, led the team, and stayed steady and confident. I would be blamed for any problems as well as receive more credit than due when things went right. I was the guy everyone looked up to and relied upon for leadership as well as making the big plays when needed most.

Running Back *Frank Mella: Ground Operations Manager; Mt. Kilimanjaro Summit Leader*

Always a critical position on a football team, the running back (there are usually two in most formations) gets the ball on plays called for him. His job is to find the open hole and advance the ball up the field. A specific hole or area may be indicated but may be occupied by a defender instead, which necessitates adjustments being made "on the fly." The running back is also sometimes called upon to block for the other running backs, or the QB on certain pass plays. In addition, he may turn into a receiver and catch a pass.

In many ways, I would consider Frank to be the MVP of the actual event/tour as he consistently outperformed expectations each and every day. Following the introduction by Sandy, I worked with him steadily, giving him missions and projects and assignments that simply needed to get done. Throughout the planning and execution of the trip, he made play after play, executing with grace, flow and professionalism. Most times he remained an unnoticed worker, but I knew he would always advance the ball.

As Managing Director of Kilele Savane, Ltd., he organizes trips on a weekly basis but had never before undertaken such a monumental project.

Running Back *Enrique Ramos: CONADEIP Official Party Director*

Every successful football team has at least two quality running backs who can 'run to daylight' when it is there, but are also able to duck their heads and get tough yards when the defense has aligned and adjusted well to stop them.

Enrique was the key man in Mexico, without whom this event would not have been possible. A bit of a breakaway threat he would make long runs when called upon to keep everything moving within CONADEIP. He was also able to grind out first downs for months and months, always with a positive attitude.

Running Back (short yardage plays) *Carmelo Ramírez: CONADEIP Assistant Director*

On every football team, there is a short yardage running back whose job it is to get the job done when needed, usually fighting hard to eke out a few inches, feet, or yards for a first down. Always a vital play, this allows the offense to retain possession, if it works, while keeping the ball moving.

Carmelo was a steady ally to Enrique who did anything and everything needed in the line of "grunt work." He would quietly take direction, do his job, and played an understated but significant role throughout the planning as well as during the event itself.

Wide Receiver *Sandy Hatfield Clubb: Drake University Director of Athletics, Team and Official Party Director*

In most football formations these days, there are three wide receivers whose primary job it is to make big plays, despite attracting tough coverage by the defense.

Sandy was the "go to" receiver who could always be counted on to make solid, critical receptions and plays. She had countless roles to play prior to and during the event and continued to successfully 'move the chains' as needed to keep things going. Certainly there were times when the entire project was in danger of being stopped and she would always find a way to keep it moving.

Slot Receiver *Jennie Phillips: Director of 'Stuff'*

The slot receiver is usually shorter in height, but runs precise routes and finds ways to get open for passes. He is often unheralded but nearly always makes big-time receptions.

Jennie works for the University of Notre Dame in the Recreational Sports Department, and has worked with me on specific events since 2005, helping to orchestrate the Notre Dame Football Fantasy Camps I created and managed 2003 to 2008. She also helped me successfully run the Notre Dame Japan Bowl in 2009, doing a superb job of taking care of our coach, Lou Holtz. She has always done great work with the coaches as well as helping me with the more technically oriented part of my business, setting up PowerPoint presentations, Excel sheets and PDF documents. For months, I told her I appreciated her help but I really didn't think I needed her on this trip. As game day (the tour itself) drew closer though, I realized how much I did need her organizational skills to keep everything and everybody coordinated, as I couldn't be in ten places at one time. She willingly joined in and did an outstanding job.

Wide Receiver *Dr. Steve Meyer: Medical Director*

The third wide receiver is as critical as the other two, often working in conjunction with the others to either get himself open for a pass completion or working as a team player to help get the other receivers open.

Steve did this from the first day we met in Iowa. He was instrumental in so many ways, beginning with the introduction to Minister Nyalandu via email and phone, which proved to be incredibly critical for the event. He also served as our Medical Director for the event, assisting with prescriptions for preventive medicines, arranging for any needed emergency help at the Arusha Lutheran Medical Center and advising throughout the course of the event. In addition to all his efforts dealing with the Kili Bowl, he worked hard to open a new orphanage just outside of Arusha, the same day as the Kili Bowl game, which will help needy children for decades to come.

Field Goal Kicker/Place Kicker *Mike Carlson: TV Announcer*

The kicker's role is simply to boot the ball through the uprights, scoring either one or three points, depending on the situation. Often this role is taken for granted, but often times these points can determine the outcome of a game.

Mike, a longtime friend of Mike Preston's, is an American who has lived in Great Britain most of his life and does a lot of work with the NFL, Channel 4, and other television networks across the UK. When we finalized our TV deal with ITV and CBS Sports Network, I realized we needed somebody who knew the sport to handle the play-by-play broadcasting for the diverse audience and Mike ended up being the perfect man for the job.

Holder for "Point after Touchdowns"/Field Goals *Dr. Luanne Freer: High Altitude Medical Specialist*

The holder must receive and set up the ball in the correct position, enabling the place kicker to be successful with his kick.

Dr. Freer, who runs an emergency medical clinic at Mt. Everest Base Camp, came to us as one of the world's foremost high altitude specialists. She provided comfort for me, the QB/organizer, and for all who would take on the mountain. We realized we had an extremely skilled person caring for any issues which could occur on Kilimanjaro, which was essential.

Punter *Tim Brockman: Videographer*

A punter's role is to "flip the field," to gain massive yardage by punting the ball to the other team. While giving the ball over to the opponent is not a goal of the offense, the punt can be a huge offensive weapon when used properly.

A talented, experienced videographer, Tim and I have worked together for over two decades, beginning with special projects for Vision Quest, a child care agency we once worked for. He has since moved to Montana, produced numerous network outdoor programs and tragically lost a leg in a motorcycle accident. When I reached out to him to join us in Tanzania he lit up, as it renewed his creative spirits and energy. He did a superb job and wholeheartedly dove into the project, referring to himself as "two cameras, one leg."

Kick Return Specialist *Alex Russiani: Mexico Team Coordinator.*

The kick returner must be quick on his feet, daring, innovative and while most often simply does his job by catching and returning the ball for a short gain, at times he gets to "break one" for a long run or even a score.

Alex is a Venezuelan American whose fluency in Spanish and English has become invaluable to me on events such as these. I originally met him while working with his parents and have found him to be extremely helpful on some of my past events in Mexico. He did very well as an official translator for the team as well as keeping the Mexican team coordinated. Always eager to take on assignments, we also took advantage of his varied talents in technology and photography, and certainly enjoyed his humor.

Game Officials *Bill Lemonnier and Crew: Mario Matos, Chris Fivek, Todd Desmond, Mark Armstrong, Jeff Holter*

Bill retired from his career as a school Principle and Assistant Superintendent and for the past 20 years has enjoyed working as a Big Ten Official. At the end of the 2010 season he officiated the BCS National Championship game between Oregon and Auburn, which Auburn won. It was amazing to have the guy who had just refereed the National Championship Game working with us in Tanzania. He did a superb job of putting together his own team of officials to help us through the event. Included in the officials' lineup were three men from Penn State I told him about who had worked at my Penn State Fantasy Football Camps in previous years. They were so committed to becoming part of the event, the paid their own way to Tanzania and officiated the game for us. Bill also chose a young man from Mexico who he had previously worked with on a few international games. Additionally, he brought in an official he knew from Poland who he had met while working football clinics in Europe.

This game was not an easy one to work, as there was a lot of give and take, and the Mexican team played a different style than Drake was accustomed to. It was also a little more physical than most games, after the whistle was blown. Needless to say, the referees had their work cut out for them, and they were definitely the right officials for the job. In this analogy, each of our Team Global members were depicted as offensive players. Throughout the event they were constantly challenged by a defensive team which I will depict here not as people, but as situations and challenges that occurred throughout the planning and execution of the event. If it were easy, everyone would do it!

Defense

Here is the defensive line-up for this particular event:

Nose Tackle *Overall Cost per traveler*

Right in the middle of the defense, in front of the Offensive Center, is the player who is usually the strongest and most stubbornly difficult to move out of the way for the offense to be able to complete the play.

The single biggest potential obstacle, once we had the teams selected and committed, was the overall cost of the event. The flights themselves were approximately $1,800, depending upon departure city, with Drake flying out of Minneapolis and CONADEIP from Houston after a bus ride from Monterrey, Mexico. Each team had to find ways to secure funding and our Team Global members managed, coordinated and assisted in this herculean effort.

In Tanzania, the offense was able to insure the event was first class and at costs that were reasonable and within budget.

Defensive Ends *Drake and CONADEIP teams' and travelers' issues*

Defensive alignments generally have three or four players directly opposite the offensive line, and are the first obstacle to overcome if the ball is to be advanced by successful plays. For this scenario, a three-man front with two of them being defensive ends is a huge issue to overcome as they are by design tall, rangy, fast and tough individuals who sack Quarterbacks and contain or limit the Running Backs by turning all plays inside.

While there were many challenging factors to this overall event, it all hinged on getting players to commit and travel, getting parental support and having the universities involved. So our Team had to attack the Defensive Ends head-on, figuring out ways to overcome their concerns and issues. Sometimes we went right at them, other times went around. While the travelers themselves were certainly not defensive, there were a myriad of issues that caused them great angst, forcing our team to use all resources available to them.

Linebackers *Flights, Stadium, Accommodations, Mountain safety*

In this alignment with three Defensive Linemen, there are four Linebackers whose job it is to make most of the tackles during the game. These are always agile, but strong men who can move laterally as well as forward and back. They know how to "read" what the offense is doing, by alignment first, and cause havoc if not attacked and blocked properly. In football scouting terminology, the various Linebackers are often referred to as the "Sam," "Mike," and "Will." These are simply men's names that share their first letters with "Strong side," "Middle," and "Weak side."

As an offensive unit, we took on the Linebackers in a multitude of ways but always with exhaustive pre-event preparation, close cooperation during the event and "adjusting with poise" as needed. Sometimes in a football game things just come up and must be dealt with, or lose yardage and ultimately, the game.

In Tanzania, losing was not an option, so we planned for each contingency, took what we thought to be the best route or option at the time, and executed as well as we could…then adjusted!

Middle Linebacker, *"Mike": Flights*

The heart and soul of a defense around which all else hinges.

While the most direct route to Tanzania is to fly from a major American gateway to Amsterdam and then on to Kilimanjaro Airport, we sought out options that might be more economical, but not make an already lengthy journey more arduous. After considering a wide breadth of alternatives, in the end the direct route still proved to be the best. Of course, getting our large number of people to and through multiple airports with football gear, baggage, school needs, and donated items (footballs and books) was not simple, but it worked!

Rover Linebacker: *Stadium*

A tough, hard-nosed, smart player.

The stadium seemed like a never ending obstacle, from finding a suitable facility, constructing an American football field (never before built in Tanzania) out of a barren soccer field, to decorating the sidelines with the hope of dressing it up a bit. We also had to make sure each element was in place, including things like the scoreboard, team rooms and restrooms. A great deal of planning and innovative thinking was needed to accomplish this task. Just as an offense must at times be creative and tenacious to get around and past tough inside linebackers, we exercised the same efforts with the field, creating a suitable environment in which to play Africa's first game of American football.

Weak side Linebacker, "Will": *Accommodations*

A linebacker who must be able to move in all directions in order to plug holes in the middle, stop outside runs, and drop into pass zones.

Finding multiple hotels in different locations for various parts of the trip took a lot of investigating and planning. We needed hotels that were reasonably priced, clean and, most of all large enough to support the number of people we were bringing with us. As it turned out I was quite pleased with what we were able to find and use for accommodations. We tried to keep teams together as much as possible but sometimes they needed to split into multiple smaller hotels. All in all, we used the services of seven hotels, tents for the mountain and safari segments of the trip, and one group of individuals stayed with host families during the community service portion of the trip.

Strong side Linebacker, "Sam": Safety and Security

Very similar in style and approach as the "Will" Linebacker, but a bit bigger, as more plays are run right at him due to the strength of the offensive formation.

Tanzania is a democratic country, which has remained quite stable and free of many of the military and guerilla problems that plague other African nations. One only needs to look at a map to see Somalia and its active rebels lie close by to the northeast. Our approach was to protect our entire group and overcome any issues that might arise, many of which would be difficult to ascertain. I traveled to Tanzania three times in advance to scout, learn and explain, met with key people like Paul Mella, Frank's cousin who was the head of military intelligence nationally and allowed our Team Tanzania allies to handle security, as they could do it best.

Defensive Backs *Political Approval, Media coverage, Ground Operations, Mount Kilimanjaro*

Once the offense feels it might have a play that is working and controlling the defensive line and linebackers, there is the last line of defense, the Defensive Backs. These are always the fastest players on the field, with amazing athletic ability whose job it is to somehow stop the offensive onslaught. At times, they may appear to be "beaten deep," only to make a spectacular play that stops the play cold, or even ends up in a turnover whereby the defense will now go on offense.

For the Kili Bowl, there were major elements that had to be handled properly, with great care, planning and personal involvement or they would simply make the event less successful, more difficult and even dangerous. These elements I define as the Defensive Backs in general, and more specifically the Cornerbacks and Safeties.

Cornerback: *Political Approval*

The "corners" are simply the defensive playmakers who, because they are highly respected, the offense will carefully and selectively run or pass to. In order to carry out the game plan, the Corners must be respected, but not feared; challenged, but not carelessly.

Tanzania is a small country in terms of the power structure and who can get what done. From the very beginning I looked at this as a fun challenge, getting to know some of the key people personally, in this nation I had known so little about. Fortunately, Lazaro Nyalandu was most gracious, happy to open doors, provide introductions and walk me through the maze of who's who in Tanzanian power. Without his help and guidance, I am sure we would have struggled much more to gain support and approval.

Cornerback: *Media Coverage*

Playing the other side of the field, the second "corner" performs the same role and needs to be handled just as carefully.

Our media coverage was a multi-faceted, multi-media effort in America, Mexico and Tanzania. The efforts for media coverage in Mexico and the US followed pretty much the same patterns and approaches that we had engaged in for various events over the years. The system in Tanzania, however, was a bit foreign to be sure. We knew we needed some media coverage ahead of the event to help attract crowds for the game and hopefully some sponsorship. Also, on a broader basis, I could not envision producing an event of this historical nature, with all we were able to embark on, without getting it onto television somehow, some way. To achieve success in this undertaking, I would again have to rely on personal connections and introductions to key players.

Strong Safety: *Ground Operations*

Being able to tackle like a Linebacker in order to stop runs, as well as play pass coverage like a Cornerback to break up passes, the Strong Safety is a man of many talents.

The logistics of getting our different groups of travelers to the various hotels, the game stadium, the assorted community service locations, safaris, and Kilimanjaro, while keeping them safe as we were driven on some of the most challenging roads I have ever encountered, was an enormous feat. Frank Mella and his team used their expertise and were able to overcome this line of defense skillfully.

Free Safety: *Mount Kilimanjaro*

The last line of defense, he is the deepest defender on a pass play and provides secondary support on a run play. He gets the advantage of standing in the back, watching the play and attacking where he believes the ball will end up. The Free Safety is also one to take risks, a gambler who cannot always be scouted and planned for accurately.

For many, Mount Kilimanjaro was the hardest part of the trip to surmount both physically and mentally. The positive energy and encouragement needed to overcome the cold, the altitude and the long days took an entire team effort. Not only did this include the individuals from the US and Mexico, but also the more than five hundred guides, porters, cooks, and other individuals whose support was invaluable to this climb.

View from the Summit

As with every team or business, the key to success is that everybody plays their role as efficiently and effectively as they can, making it a true team effort. This group of individuals performed admirably, enabling the Global Kilimanjaro Bowl to run seamlessly. Without each one of them, this event could never have been completed to the same level of success that we accomplished.

Every event brings its own set of defensive obstacles that my teams have to overcome. While I have organized and produced over 130 other football events around the world, they were only similar to the Kili Bowl in broad parameters, as the specific details were utterly unique. Every game and event is different, but this one more so than any other I had ever done.

6

We Have No Breaking Point! (Ara's most memorable quote)

How do managers, coaches, teachers, administrators, even doctors get everybody on their various teams to head in the same direction, to commit to achieving the overall goal, regardless of what it takes? By this, I mean not only having their team members get their individual portion of the work done, but doing it all together with the same amount of passion and enthusiasm as their leaders?

I believe that the most critical key is to take the dreams, goals, and objectives of the leaders and make them personal for each individual on the team! Leaders, truly successful ones, are able to communicate their goals to everyone on the team, have them take personal pride in the overall achievement, and make it their own dream.

Then, make it clear through example that failure Is not an option; have no breaking point. No longer should workers focus as employers and employees or coaches and players, as all are working together, reaching for the same goal.

You have created your team, but now it is time to develop their dream.

Local kids with buckets and helmet

The real story behind the Global Kilimanjaro Bowl is the fact that we brought young men from Mexico and Iowa halfway around the world to unite with the Tanzanian people. Three different cultures, three different countries, three different peoples all combining efforts to help the local people of Tanzania build and improve orphanages, schools, nurseries, playgrounds and sports fields, plant trees and help provide a supply of clean water. In addition, they would share in a unique sporting experience for the first time ever in Africa, and top it all off by climbing to the rooftop of Africa. To me, this was such a compelling story for any business or organization that I believed corporate America would jump at the opportunity to be a part of it.

At this stage, I now had the smoothly functioning team at Drake University, and the similar team in Mexico. I had my Tanzanian team more or less constructed and Team Global was ready and willing to go. The question then became, how would each team's "coach/manager" get his/her people motivated, willing, even hungry to take on the enormous quantity of work necessary to make this materialize?

In October of 2010, we knew everybody involved wanted the event to happen, but there were still numerous huge barriers that needed to be overcome. The main obstacle on everybody's mind was how they would obtain the finances to cover the trip. At a cost of approximately $4,000 per person, this was the most expensive tour I had priced to date. I was concerned about the students being able to raise the money, as I believe almost everybody was. Securing the funds would take a great deal of time, effort, and teamwork. But I knew that Coach Creighton, Enrique and Sandy wanted this event to come to fruition as badly as I did and that they would find a way to get it done.

It was amazing how everyone involved worked religiously to find the needed funds. I experienced my own difficulties trying to find sponsors for the event so I would not lose money myself. I was often reminded that asking for donations and sponsors was not as easy as it sounded. However, with the Herculean efforts by Team Drake, Team Mexico, Team Global as well as Team IRIS, the event costs were covered by the time we were on our flights to Tanzania.

Team Drake

Team Drake was highly motivated from the very beginning and while they knew it was a costly event, they were not willing to give up on something that most people could only dream about. Throughout this entire process Drake proved that with preparation, teamwork, sacrifice and competitive will, they could make anything happen.

Drake had to raise over $350,000 to make the trip a reality! By the time they embarked from Tanzania the team had received money from over eight hundred donors to whom the players shared the task in writing thank you notes on their plane ride home. The greatest single gift they received was $16,000, but as Coach Creighton explains, "I don't want to discount anything, as we were appreciative of every penny, because it was pennies that added up to make the $350,000."

One of the promises the Athletic Department made to the university when they knew they had to raise this large sum of money was that they would not ask donors who normally give to the Bulldog Club or any other university-related club or event. They wanted to avoid taking any money away from their operating budget or other yearly promotions. Therefore, all of the money had to come from new donors. While difficult to do at first, it has now proven to be extremely helpful to Drake Athletics. The University was able to bring in some donors and alumni who had never given to Drake Athletics before, but wanted to give to this unique, and special project. Many of these donors have continued to provide support long after the Kili Bowl, which has improved the university's overall fundraising efforts.

The Drake University football team started their fundraising initiative during the 2010 regular season when they asked fans to sponsor them and donate money based on the number of points scored or sacks the defense made. This particular attempt wasn't as successful as they had hoped, but in January 2011 one of the team's defensive tackles, Paddy O'Connell, worked hard to organize another fundraising event, a Lift-a-Thon. For this event players asked people to sponsor them for lifting weights. It turned out to be a great success and generated

$104,000. The reality of being able to raise this amount got the players excited and motivated to continue working toward their financial goals.

Beyond these team fundraising activities, the individual players took it upon themselves to find more money. By the time the trip rolled around, Coach Creighton was proud of his team and their ability to work together to reach their goal. "There were some guys," Chris recalled, "who raised over $10,000 knowing it would only cost them $4,000, and there were others who worked really hard at it and were only able to raise $1,500. Those who were able to raise more than $4,000 knew that they were raising it for their teammates. It wasn't just giving a guy ten bucks for dinner, it was 'I have raised $6,000, and I am going for $4,000 more' and then giving this to a guy who could be beating him out of his position next year. The dynamic of teamwork was absolutely phenomenal. You were talking about significant sums of money and everybody who wanted to go on the trip actually got to go. They all took care of each other."

Even the coaches took care of one another. Coach Creighton and some others were adamant that they would pay their own way. They felt that they weren't going to ask their players to do something if they weren't willing to do it themselves. Though some of the younger coaches were eager and excited to join this event, they just didn't have the funds to travel, so the university worked hard to help cover their costs. None of the coaches ever took for granted that they would be going on this amazing experience to Africa. In fact, one coach came to Coach Creighton's office in February 2011 and, with doors closed, discussed how much he would love to be a part of this trip. However, he had seriously deliberated for some time and had decided that if it would be better for somebody else on staff to go, that they could have his spot. Thankfully, the university was ultimately able to secure enough funds so that not one coach who wanted to go would be left out.

The person who was put in charge of collecting and organizing all of the money the students brought in was the athletics department business manager, Sue Tygeson. Though Sue initially had some feelings of doubt toward being able to raise all of the money for the event, she proved to be an incredibly supportive person and was willing to help in any way she could. With students bringing her $10 here and $150 there, it would have been easy to make mistakes, but Sue kept everything well organized with assorted spreadsheets that would perplex most people. Seeing the players on a regular basis, she was also able to get to know them on a personal level. She became incredibly engaged in the entire process, as the student athletes would share their fundraising stories with her. She would often relay the stories to Sandy with tears in her eyes, profoundly impressed and proud of these young men. Sue wasn't able to go on the trip, but as Sandy fondly remembered, "I became a really big part of the team."

Throughout the entire event Drake had to follow NCAA rules, and that included regulations regarding fundraising. One of the rules stated that all of the money Drake received for the event had to go into a pool and be distributed equally to the players. Coach Creighton had called the team together to clarify the rule, as the event drew closer, and all of the money still wasn't in. He had posed the question to the NCAA, "What if the money comes up a little short? Would they have to decide who could come on the trip and who couldn't?" To which the NCAA replied that in that case the tour wouldn't be possible. Every player who wanted to go had to have the opportunity, and if they weren't able to secure the funds, the university would have to cover it or the trip would have to be cancelled.

Really? Ah, the wisdom of the NCAA.

Drake's fundraising attempts went down to the wire. By the end of April, they were still thousands of dollars short. Sandy met with the Board of Trustees, explaining to them that the overall project was expensive but so very worthwhile. She also related numerous success stories of the student athletes and the money they had raised. She explained how they were making it work but that there were surprise costs that kept coming up such as tips that they would have to pay to the porters and tour guides, as well as advance medical expenses to ensure the students' safety. She never asked the Board for money, but merely wanted to explain the situation to keep them in the loop. At the end of the meeting though, one of the trustees came up to her and handed her a check for $7,500 to help with expenses. Later that day, another trustee came up and handed her another check for $7,500. She told the generous person that the money had already been given to her earlier, but the donor insisted that he still wanted to donate the money. In that one meeting alone, Sandy was able to raise $15,000, without really asking! As she recalled, "That's the thing about this project, it was just so unique and special that a broad base of people wanted to help."

Team Mexico

As Dr. Mijares wisely put it when team Mexico first signed onto the event, "If you believe in the value of any difficult project, you will overcome the obstacles." Team Mexico found this to be especially true when it came to fundraising. To start out, every one of the six participating Tec campuses represented on the team roster offered $10,000. Providing a kick-start to their fundraising efforts they already had $60,000 in the bank, which definitely helped to get everyone else on board with doing their share. Each student then went out to raise his own money, either through getting jobs, asking neighbors, doing car washes, or simply asking their parents and relatives. They had each committed to raising about $1,000, which brought in roughly $40,000 total from the student's share. So, with $100,000 committed, Enrique knew obtaining the rest of the money wouldn't be impossible.

Enrique also had a uniquely talented young woman named Zuleika on his team, who worked at one of the Tec Monterrey campuses located in Mexico City. Her primary job relating to this event was to find sponsors, pure and simple. As with others, she totally believed in the project and was able to relay that belief to her potential donors. Throughout the process she found that it wasn't extremely difficult to find people to donate money because, as she has explained to Enrique, "When I have a good project for the university, the people will say yes."

While the team's approach to fundraising was well organized and shared by everybody involved, Dr. Mijares ultimately helped them overcome their final obstacle by securing the remainder of the monies needed. Talk about a team leader!

Team IRIS

The entire year before the event, not only was Drake University soliciting donations for the Kili Bowl throughout Iowa, but so were the folks at the Iowa-based nonprofit organization, IRIS. Led by Del Christensen, the Iowa Resource for International Service group was more than eager to perform a critical role within the parameters of the Kili Bowl. While the football teams had raised money to cover their logistical expenses, IRIS undertook its own fundraising campaign to raise money as well as inkind donations to support the nineteen volunteer projects the two teams would participate in while in Tanzania. Amazingly, they reached out to everybody they could without stepping on the toes of Drake's fundraising efforts. The single largest fundraising effort IRIS had ever undertaken, they were ultimately able to raise over $30,000 in cash, on top of other in-kind donations. This money would eventually be invested wisely in Tanzania for everything from the bricks and mortar used to build school walls, to the tools for painting, digging and building, to the five hundred trees planted by the student athletes. Most of the money came to them in the form of $25 to $50 individual donations, with another $2,000 to $3,000 from individual corporations. It just proved Coach Creighton's point that "every penny counts."

Team Global

When I originally priced this event for the two teams, I knew there would be very little margin in the cost per person, but I was fearful that the fee each had to pay could be so high it may discourage them from traveling. Plus, having not yet traveled to Tanzania when I set the price, I simply had to estimate many of the costs. However, all along I figured that certainly some corporation(s) would see the benefits of this event and want to provide their support for it.

Unfortunately and surprisingly, I found the event to be an extremely difficult sell. In the end, my efforts proved highly unproductive, considering the amount of time and energy I put into finding a sponsor.

I began by reaching out to organizations I thought would look at this event as an opportunity for international expansion and growth of the sport. These organizations included the National Football League, the American Football Coaches Association, USA Football, and the International Federation of Football. Regrettably, none of them seemed to share my vision.

Then I looked toward apparel and equipment manufacturers such as Nike, Under Armour, Wilson, Adidas, Russell, Puma, and Reebok. Surely, with their worldwide investment and commensurate revenue from the sport of football, this would be worthy of their involvement. They weren't interested either.

I thought approaching a turf company to install an artificial turf field that would be drought resistant, perfect for the Tanzania dry and rainy seasons, and would be used by the athletes in Tanzania long after we left was a reasonable idea. I reached out to leaders at Field Turf, AstroTurf, Pro Grass…all companies where I knew employees at high levels whom I had met through other events I had worked on in the past. For the most part, they took a serious look at the project, but after deliberating over it for some time they all came up with the same reasons why not—it was too big of a project, it was too risky, too strange, too unique, oh, and it was the first time.

My frustration built as I quickly began to understand why a lot of things don't happen for the first time. It was just not that easy to convince organizations to support something brand new, let alone one that would be staged in Africa! Most decision makers, I discovered, were cautious to a fault. Why risk their job or receive criticism for something new and dynamic and worthwhile when the safe decision was just to keep moving ahead as always?

One of my goals for the children attending our planned football clinics in the days leading up to the game in Arusha was for each one of them to receive an American football. I estimated that there would be around a thousand youngsters ages twelve to seventeen attending and learning, so I went out to look for a company to donate the footballs. I ended up asking each of the ball manufacturing companies, Wilson, Nike (again), Spalding, Rawlings, Baden, and anyone else I could find who might have direct access to footballs. Astonishingly, none of them wanted to help!

We could not show up in Tanzania, promoting and playing American football, interacting with and showing children how to play the game, and not give them anything. Frustrated at the lack or support in this area, I ended up personally purchasing Baden brand rubber footballs through a dealer in Arizona who gave me a favorable price of $5 per ball. Another $5,000 unbudgeted expense, but simply the right thing to do. I couldn't help but think how this would have adversely affected the profit structure of a Nike or Spalding or Rawlings. Or perhaps positively!

I soon found out that another difficult issue surrounding the donated footballs wasn't necessarily just purchasing them, but then determining how we would transport them from the US to Tanzania, all the while avoiding the cost and risk of international shipping and customs? The two teams helped out tremendously with this as I sent half to Drake and the other half to Houston, Texas. At Drake, Coach Creighton organized it so that each staff member and player put seven deflated balls in their individual bags to fly to Tanzania. The other four hundred that went to Houston were actually sent to a friend of mine who in turn transported them to the airport where he met the Mexican team bus the day of their flight. As the team disembarked from the bus, he pulled the boxes of deflated footballs from his van. The team had been told to leave about five pounds worth of extra space in their bags so they could carry these balls. Each traveler then jammed eight of them into their bags, as I am sure other curious travelers gazed on.

Every bit of this extra effort was ultimately well worth it. What a memory for us all, to see the smiling faces of the children playing with them at the clinics, and then in the stadium at halftime of the Kili Bowl game. To this day, those thousand rubber footballs are being tossed and kicked around by the youth of Tanzania, surely providing a fun activity and bringing smiles to their faces.

My last major endeavor to obtain sponsorship support was to contact the big multinational companies like Coca-Cola. Surely Coke, a worldwide brand, hugely popular in developing countries where their ads are ubiquitous, would see the benefit of helping with the event.

If not them, then one of their competitors like Pepsi, or even one of the various sports drinks companies like Gatorade. I discovered that in these companies, if I made it past the first line of defense without receiving a definitive no, that I would then get bounced around between the various marketing divisions. The person in the US would say, "Well, it's a nice idea, but it's happening in Africa and we don't really have an African budget." Or, "I don't see a place for it in our department but let me check with our Mexico Division and maybe they'll be able to help you." Then, the Mexico Division would get back to me, after multiple calls and emails, only to tell me, "We don't really have funding for anything in Africa, if it were in Mexico, or if it were soccer, it would be a different story." The few companies like Coca-Cola, that did have African budgets, merely said, "No, it doesn't fit our model."

It just didn't seem to fit anybody's "model." Talk about frustration; I spent a lot of late nights sending emails, petitioning men and women at all levels, trying to find a sponsor, with very little return.

I can't leave out the fact that, thankfully, there were two companies who did help out and invest in the event. The first was a group called Younger Optics, an optic lens company with whom I had a connection to through my friend, Keith Cross. Younger Optics was able to provide some cash, which we were grateful to receive, as well as two hundred pairs of new sunglasses for all of our travelers, which was quite a nice bonus for the players. The other company, with whom a longtime friend of mine, John Green, connected me, was Rogers Athletic. They sell football equipment for fields and training, and agreed to provide all of the football game needs for the field and sidelines including chains, first down markers, yardsticks, pylons, and yard markers. These additions made the field look like a real football game was being played, as it was. They donated all of this gear and shipped some of it to Tanzania while our travelers hauled the remainder in their personal luggage. I remain greatly appreciative that these two companies were willing to step up to the plate, seize the opportunity, helping us make the Kili Bowl so successful.

Through all the effort expended trying to find sponsors, I got a really good sense of how hard it was to do something new. An American football game in Tanzania was extremely unique, and it wasn't like it was the University of Texas or the Green Bay Packers. This event was the next level below, as it was Drake University and the CONADEIP all-stars. Those other, larger teams would never take on an event like this, as it wouldn't generate enough revenue. This event wasn't about generating revenue; it was about experiential education, about doing something special for the young athletes who traveled and for the people they encountered. The corporate world, unfortunately, doesn't always see the long-term benefit in that. At least they didn't in this case.

After working hard the previous year and being told no by football teams and leagues and federations around the world, and then being turned down by potential sponsors of all kinds, I was even more determined to make this event work. I believed that when one of those teams or companies decided not to be a part of the event that one of two things had occurred: either I just didn't explain it well or properly enough to make my dream a dream of theirs, or I didn't get the idea in front of the right person at the right time.

In today's world, it's not necessarily about the idea, which could be brilliant! It is about getting that idea to the right ears and eyes. Within every company and organization there are people looking for great opportunities, who might be inclined to say yes. But they are all too often surrounded by multiple layers of people whose job, they believe, is to say no…to defend the turf, to watch the budgets, to follow the guidelines. To me those people are the ones who stop innovation.

So, in retrospect, I accept that it was my fault for not finding the right people, for not communicating my dream, in the correct manner, to make it their dream.

While I wasn't able to receive much financial help from companies in the US, I continued to seek help in Tanzania. Tourism, being the number one industry in Tanzania, would benefit substantially from an event like this, bringing a large amount of both American and Mexican money to Tanzania. While I thought it might be possible to get some help from companies in Tanzania, or another African nation, the reality remained that this is a poor continent overall. There were companies and organizations profiting from their work, but by and large there simply were not large marketing budgets, especially when compared to US companies that had been so reticent to invest.

I went to the local Arusha-based bottler that handled bottled water and beer, both huge industries in the country. No success.

I then went to the mobile phone companies whose ads are visible everywhere throughout the streets of Tanzania. I was turned down.

I was also able to secure meetings during my scouting trips with dozens of companies involved in travel, manufacturing, agriculture, etc. No luck.

My final shot was to go to the Tanzania National Parks Association (TANAPA). A large portion of the cost for each of the travelers would be the parks fees. The fee to climb Mt. Kilimanjaro alone was substantial, about $625 per person, on top of the fees to enter each of the National Parks we visited on the safaris. In an effort to hopefully recuperate some of those fees, I created a proposal, through the help and with direction of Lazaro. In the proposal, I explained that we were not only going to bring a large group of people and money into the country through this event but that we would also bring plenty of visibility and promotion for the Tanzanian National Parks. A TV show would air on the CBS Sports Network after the event. There would also be extensive articles published in various magazines. Basically, they would receive free publicity in three countries. In return, I requested discounted parks fees for our travelers. After putting this proposal together in January, I sent it to Lazaro so he might review and comment. He read through it and told me he thought it was a reasonable request. He then went on to explain to me how to present the information as well as to whom at TANAPA.

Later that month, I made my second trip to Tanzania and met with Mr. Lukong Mhandagani, the board member Lazaro recommended I talk to, to discuss the proposal. He was a rather engaging, large man who seemed to believe what I was proposing to be a reasonable request, and offered to refer it to their Executive Director in Arusha. Lazaro said he would also forward it to him. It sounded to me like this was a very positive step.

I wasn't going to hold my breath for anything to happen until I returned again to Tanzania. I had found it very difficult to do business with individuals in Tanzania over the phone or through e-mail. The time difference made it difficult to communicate in real time. Also, while the Tanzanians were extremely friendly and willing to meet and help in person, e-mails did not seem to create the same sense of urgency as they do here in the States. On top of that, I felt it would be better to meet the Executive Director face to face to properly explain the proposal to him and make it more personal. Therefore, after the proposal was sent, I requested a meeting in March, via email, to which he graciously agreed.

I then decided, before I headed over to Tanzania for my third and final scouting trip, that my goal would be to get the fees reduced by about half, about $300 per person for the two hundred people on the trip, which would be a fair amount of money.

While the TANAPA Executive Director Alan Kijaze had said he would love to get together with me, we never actually got around to arranging a meeting before my arrival. Both Lazaro and I tried to contact him for a meeting date before my trip, but with no luck. In March I showed up in Tanzania with numerous missions, as there remained many items to finalize before the two teams would arrive two months later. The most critical goal of this trip, however, was to meet with Mr. Kijaze. For the five days that I was there I continued to try and get a hold of him, but received no reply to my emails, texts, and calls. I was frustrated at this point as this meeting was, from a business standpoint, one of the key reasons for me to embark on this scouting trip.

Finally, on the day I was supposed to return to the States, Lazaro contacted me and told me I had a meeting set with Kijaze for 4:00 p.m. My flight home was to depart at 8:00 p.m. We met in the lobby of the Arusha Hotel, a well-known property and business center popularized in the John Wayne movie *Hatari*. The lobby was one of the most active I have seen for business meetings and where the Who's Who in Arusha came together to talk.

That day we were able to go over the proposal together as he listened intently to my ideas. I went through each point, telling him what I could offer and what I was requesting in exchange, which was a reduction in the fares and rates. He ultimately told me, "You know this seems very reasonable, seems like a great program, I believe we will be able to help you. Let me take this to our board meeting in two weeks to get final approval, but this looks very good to me."

At that moment, I was heartened by the fact that we could be looking at a reduction of somewhere around $60,000 in the total cost. Now, mind you, as the event moved along from the planning stages in May of 2010 when I initially set the price at $4,000 per traveler, everything, except for the fixed land price that I had set with Frank Mella, had increased in cost. Some costs increased substantially. You should also understand that I am not a great accounting guy. Call it bad business practice, but I have neither the time nor the interest to sit down and figure out the detailed expenses of every single item on each event far ahead of time. I know I should, but I would rather spend my time coming up with ideas, handling the production side, marketing my events and making sure all runs smoothly, than counting the dollars. Costs that I had not originally accounted for included: the extra scouting trip I found I had to take (I had only planned for two originally), the increased price in flights, my two trips to Mexico, my two trips to Drake, securing a TV package, getting a TV producer, security, and on and on. In the end, everything cost more than I had expected.

On my flight home I did some quick math to figure out the actual ballpark price of the event and discovered that the bestcase scenario was a breakeven for Global Football, that is, if we were able to reduce the TANAPA costs. A more reasonable scenario, if those costs weren't reduced, was that I would lose between $60,000 and $80,000. I started realizing this potential loss when I wasn't able to find any sponsors, but as bad as the numbers sounded, I certainly wasn't going to back out at this point!

Due to my commitment to Coach Creighton, Sandy, the Drake football players, Enrique, CONADEIP, everyone who had gone out for months before the trip raising money, the people of Tanzania, and the IRIS folks to whom we had committed doing service work... backing out was *not* an option. I convinced myself that if we didn't get any money I would chalk it off as a great once-in-a-lifetime event that provided the student athletes with an incredible opportunity, and one that allowed my wife, Janet, and me to go to Africa, meet some wonderful people, witness amazing sights and conquer a lifetime dream of mine by climbing Mt. Kilimanjaro.

Now, after returning home, I was excited to know that I might reclaim some of this likely event financial "loss." As the tour date drew closer I became more apprehensive, as I never was able to reach the TANAPA Executive Director again directly. I left phone messages, I sent emails, and I even tried to reach him through Lazaro and Frank Mella. But nothing. I didn't hear a word. Finally, in mid-May, the day came for me to leave for Tanzania, nine days ahead of everyone else, realizing there would be a myriad of final details to cover in person. I wanted to arrive early to manage all of the last minute details I would have to go over in Tanzania and only hoped I would be able to get a hold of Mr. Kijaze during those final days.

Janet drove me to the Dallas/Fort Worth airport, a little over an hour from the house. I was running a bit late because I needed to make sure everything was taken care of in my office before heading out to Africa for more than three weeks. I figured I could get to the airport an hour and a half before the flight and I would be safe. As can happen on DFW highways, there was traffic and construction, but I was determined. We even tried to skip around the traffic, four-wheeling it a few times across medians and exit ramps. I got to the terminal just forty-five minutes before the flight was supposed to depart, only to discover that the flight was closed. Despite my pleading with the airline staff, there seemed to be no talking my way into boarding. I had no alternative but to go back home.

The next day I returned to the airport with hours to spare this time, so I grabbed a bite to eat for lunch, and headed to the men's restroom before boarding the seven-hour flight to Amsterdam, then transfer for the eight-hour trip to Tanzania. There I was sitting in a DFW restroom stall with two carry-on bags, doing my business when my phone rang. I essentially run my entire Global Football operation through my cell phone, but there are limits as to when I will answer calls…that is… until I looked at it and the phone display read "TANAPA." I quickly answered the phone with a "Yes, sir, this is Patrick."

The voice on the other end was that of Mr. Kijaze, who replied, "Ahh, Patrick, how are you? I see you are coming to Tanzania."

While avoiding telling him about my current awkward situation, I responded, "Yes, I am, a day late though. I hoped to meet with you today, but I will be there tomorrow."

"No worries" he replied. "I just want you to know the Board approved your proposal last night. TANAPA will be involved in supporting your efforts. Just let me know when you get here and we will get together."

That phone call in the men's room of Terminal D at DFW airport changed the entire financial end of the event, taking it from being a serious money-losing event to nearly break-even for me. Something I will never forget and just one of the many serendipitous things that happened in and around the Kili Bowl.

View from the Summit

> Often the most memorable things take place when we least expect anything to occur, and may have about given up. And the funniest personal anecdotes are those that come at us totally out of left field, when we are least prepared. Most often good news comes when it seems there is no way it might, when I relax, accept my limitations and realize it is really not *my* will that matters.

7

Adjust with Poise

"Has anyone ever told you, you might be mad?!"

Game Day

From the very beginning, I knew the Global Kilimanjaro Bowl would be an event that should be broadcast on television, at least back in the States, but possibly in Mexico, Tanzania and elsewhere as well. My initial thoughts were to get in touch with the Discovery Network, National Geographic, the Travel Channel and other similar networks. I also believed that ESPN or one of their subsidiaries, would be interested in carrying an event such as this. To me, broadcasting the first game ever in Africa would be a tremendous opportunity for someone, a "no brainer." Ah, but whenever I believe something is a no brainer, often times it only turns out to be a brilliant idea in my brain!

Again, I must not have presented the proposal well enough or in the right light because ESPN turned me down quickly, as did Fox Sports, and National Geographic, to name a few. My first glimpse of hope came early on in the planning phase during a call with Chris Creighton, when he informed me that his father-in-law, an attorney in Houston, knew a television producer who could likely handle this type of challenge.

I immediately seized upon this opportunity, had an initial conversation with the producer, at which time he told me that he believed he would be able to get the event on the Discovery Network. He had apparently done a special with Discovery in the past that involved a charitable effort, and through this he had high level contacts with the network. He thought this would be an ideal fit for them, as did I. Finally, someone in the broadcast arena who, like me, believed this should be on the air. For the better part of that year I went back and forth with this LA-based producer, round and round, sharing ideas about the storyline and getting rough budgets from him with promises of sketchy, soft commitments of funding for the project. Throughout the entire process, he seemed to be evasive when it came to the nuts and bolts of the project, but I continued to forge onward thinking that if he had connections as he stated, this could turn out to be pretty spectacular.

Where we began to disagree, was when he wanted to make this event a competition throughout. He explained to me that would be the story television wanted to show. We would obviously have a competition when it came to the football game, but he wanted that competition to extend to the community service work. We would judge which team could complete the most service work in the time allotted.

We could turn the climb up Mount Kilimanjaro into a race to see which team made it to the top in the shortest amount of time with the highest percentage of players. It would be like "The Amazing Race-Kili Style."

I couldn't fathom turning this into one big competition, and knew Coach Creighton would not embrace the idea either, so I told him no. There was only going to be a contest for three hours during the actual game. Beyond that, the two teams would come together as one, working toward the good of Tanzania and further developing teamwork along the way. I could tell this guy didn't like my idea, but nonetheless if it was going to get on TV, the final story would be told in the editing, and I felt certain that I could get my way when we got into post-production. My key concern at this point was simply to get the event shot, the sound recorded, and the whole project developed for broadcast.

As time grew closer for the actual journey, about ninety days out, I told him it was time to put up or shut up. We needed some hard budgets, agreements and sources of funding, as well as a schedule for shooting which would impact flights, hotels and operations. As always he was elusive, but confident, indicating that these details would be forthcoming very soon.

Following that conversation, he simply went underground, disappeared; we had no communication whatsoever. I never heard from him again. Saying that, I didn't chase him down either. Through this unpleasant experience of spending way too much time trying to arrange a deal with him, I realized that I did not wish to communicate with him again. I can't stand people who waste my time with ideas and empty promises, but never deliver. If you cannot do something just tell me, and we will adjust with poise, but *don't* keep leading me on. Curiously, of the hundreds of names involved in the entire Kilimanjaro Bowl project, his name escapes me to this day, and I have no interest in searching notes to find it. Some things, and people, are just better left behind.

Fortunately, I did have serious concerns about this guy early on; believing he just wasn't going to pull through for us, and I had begun working on a backup plan. Ten weeks out from the event I contacted an old buddy of mine, Tim Brockman. We originally met in the early 1980s, when we were both working for Vision Quest, a juvenile delinquency treatment program focused on reshaping at-risk youth through hard work and responsibility. Often seen by the juvenile court system as an alternative to incarceration, we would take these teenagers on wagon train trips in the Arizona desert as well as teach them how to "break" wild mustangs, and how to survive in the wilderness of New Mexico.

Tim came into the picture when he was asked to help produce a BBC feature called *Running Wild*, focusing on "wild horses" and "wild kids." At the time I was a program manager, overseeing some twenty-four Cuban refugees based on the VQ ranch in Elfrida, Arizona. Tim was extremely talented, and fun to be around, which was especially helpful given the type of work I was doing then.

Then in the early 1990s my career took me to Fort Worth, Texas, where I worked as the Director of Corporate Development for the National Cutting Horse Association. Tim and I continued to stay in touch, producing a number of ESPN Cutting Horse specials together. When I left to start Global Football in 1996 he had moved up to Montana, and we lost track of each other for about fifteen years, until I reached out to him concerning the Kili Bowl. While I knew that he had never actually produced an American football game before, I also knew that Tim had an excellent eye for landscape, animals and sports and that he was eager for work. Sadly he had lost a leg, and almost his life, in a motorcycle accident about a decade before, so he had not done much production work in many years. He was thrilled when I asked him, and he ended up being the perfect man for the job.

Now that I had a cameraman/director for the event, I reached out to the CBS Sports Network about the project. They were new, looking for interesting programming, and upon hearing my proposal told me they would broadcast a one-hour highlight package if we produced and brought it to them. Step one accomplished!

Tim and I had agreed upon a fair fee for his services. I realized that we did not have the budget to hire an entire crew to shoot the football game, so I figured if we could attempt to interest a network in Tanzania to shoot and air the game then we might use that footage, along with Tim's single camera shots, for the program.

Once again I went to my friend Lazaro and asked, "How can we get this done?" I had related the importance of this media coverage to him, the value it would have for Tanzania overall and for many years to come. He completely agreed. Lazaro explained that there was one man he knew of, Dr. Reginald Mengi, Chairman of IPP Media who owned the largest private television network in Tanzania. Lazaro termed him the "Ted Turner of Tanzania." In addition to the TV network he owned a few radio stations, internet groups, newspapers, magazines, and the like. While Lazaro knew of him and had met him on occasion, it would take some perseverance to secure a personal meeting for me.

He did, in fact, secure a meeting, in the classic Tanzanian style to which I had become accustomed. During my last planning trip to Tanzania I received a call from Lazaro while at the Sea Cliff Hotel at about 11 am, preparing for my afternoon meetings. He directing me to get a jacket and tie on as he would pick me up at 11:30. We were to have lunch with Mr. Mengi at his house. No problem, adjust with poise, I thought.

Mr. Mengi lived in a very clean, nice looking two-story gated house with a glassed-in dining deck on the rooftop. Not huge or ostentatious by any means but quite handsomely appointed and tidy. Mr. Mengi was of Indian decent, as are many of the people in Tanzania. He also had an Indian butler who met us at the door. The barefooted man led us into the living room where we waited some ten minutes for our host to enter. I gazed around and noticed that, for the first time since I had met him, Lazaro appeared nervous. I sat there prepared, with my Drake helmet and football ready, which I always carried with me when I met folks in Tanzania. These always served as icebreakers, as well as conversation pieces. They were so rare to almost everyone I encountered that a conversation about football and the upcoming event began instantly. They also proved to be fun photo props, as many of the men I met would squeeze their head and hair into the helmet, smile and allow me to take a picture.

I set the Drake helmet on the glass coffee table, started looking around, and realized the windows in the doors were all beautiful stained glass. There was also a gorgeous marble fireplace in the next room. The house was nicely furnished, no clutter at all.

Mr. Mengi finally entered the room. He was sharply dressed in a grey suit and tie, a fairly short man, maybe in his mid-sixties, with a big smile. He came right over to us, shook our hands and sat next to me on the couch—a bit uncomfortably close by American standards. He then asked me directly, "Tell me what you want to do."

I told him about the event, as clearly and succinctly as possible. Who was coming, where they were from, how hard they had worked to earn money for the trip, what American football was in layman's terms, the community service project, the safaris, plans to summit Kilimanjaro… everything. He seemed keenly interested.

Finally, as I got to the end of my five-minute soliloquy he slapped me on the thigh, laid back with a hearty laugh, and said, "Ah, Patrick, has anybody told you, you might be mad?"

I laughed along, not quite sure where to go with this response and said, "Yes, my wife tells me that quite often."

He laughed further. At that point, I could tell he liked the project.

We went on to discuss various aspects of the event. I did try to gear the conversation toward whether or not he thought he could help me on the television deal and the various parameters concerned with it. He quickly noted that he would not be making any such decisions, that he left those up to his people who ran the various divisions and departments within his many businesses. He did tell us that he would be happy to contact the lady in charge and give her my name as well as recommend that we meet. So while it wasn't a done deal, I sure felt good about the whole thing.

After concluding our conversation on the couch, we made our way upstairs to the roof of his home. The entire roof, about sixty feet by sixty feet, was covered in Astroturf making it very comfortable to walk around. In the middle of the roof, there was a stylish glass gazebo. We walked inside the air conditioned space where there were two tables set for our meal. His son, Abdiel, also joined us for lunch, as he added insightful comments and questions to the gathering. The conversation was enjoyable, switching between American football, the Kili Bowl, and discussing happenings in America and Tanzania. I am glad I was able to spend time getting to know Mr. Mengi, as I found him to be an extremely friendly and engaging man.

From that day forward, when it had to do with television, I dealt primarily with Joyce Luhanga, the Director of Sales and Marketing at Mr. Mengi's ITV Independent Television, LTD. Joyce was engaging and highly professional to work with. She quickly replied that she would be able to help, and we continued to work together throughout the entire project.

Between Mr. Mengi's television network and Tim's hard work, we were able to capture some amazing footage of the entire event. With each segment well documented and a great support team of Tim, his editor Sean, and all those from the Tanzanian ITV network, we were able to put together a final agreement with CBS Sports Network to produce an hour special. The program aired with great reviews in the fall of 2011 and later received the 2012 Tanzania Tourist Board TV Broadcast Award at the Africa Travel Association's Presidential Forum on Tourism. In addition, the live broadcast of the game itself was available to and able to be seen by over a hundred million viewers across Africa, the Middle East, Asia, and Australia!

View from the Summit

> Those of us who like to create things, who come up with novel ideas and share them with others, encounter a wide variety of folks along the journey. Some of them are also dreamers, but not necessarily the kind that accomplish much or who will help us achieve our goals. I often find it difficult to sift through the array of people I encounter, as I find myself simply believing that everyone has good and honorable intentions.
>
> Then we also meet some very talented, focused men and women, often when we least expect it, who quickly grasp

a hold of our dreams and ideas and eagerly help us. These moments, these people are what keep life so interesting and fascinating. I continue to seek them, and thank God when I do find them.

8

JR + Muhammad + Andre = Game Stadium

In my business, as in most, we simply have to be resourceful. The nature of what we do is such that roles, tasks, budgets and plans are not readily defined, easily figured out, or even simple to adapt. That is what I like, what gets me excited about my work! I never want to be bored, and always want to do the best possible job for my clients. Yes, this is often a challenge.

John Roslien

One of the main issues with producing an American football game in a country that had never experienced American football was that while we could bring over the coaches, players, equipment, even some fans… almost everything from the US, but we could not bring a field. Well, we could have, but more on that later.

That is why, on my first scouting trip to Tanzania, I started looking immediately for a suitable field/stadium. As you may recall, the first field I visited in Moshi could have been workable, and I was told it would be in better condition once some rain fell. Saying that, when I returned for my next scouting trip in January I expected that there would at least be a little more grass. I trusted the stadium manager who had promised that the coming seasonal rains would solve this issue. However, that did not seem to be the case.

On my second scouting trip, the field was even dustier than before, giving me very little hope for improvement before game day, just a couple months away. The excuse this time around was that there had just been some sort of fair with a lot of people on the field. Now this may have been true, but how could I trust that we would have grass come game day? I knew field conditions in Tanzania were probably not going to be what we were used to in the United States, but I couldn't bring two teams halfway around the world to play on dirt. I quickly looked to my trusted friend, Frank, and said, "This will not work, we need to move on and find something better."

There always appears to be a critical point, in any event I manage, and in fact, in most every major decision involving facilities or people, when I can only believe and have faith that things will be different, for just so long. In general, I am a very trusting person, but there does come a point where I must look at the situation more critically and simply say, 'enough,' it's time to move on.

I did have a concern from the beginning that the amount of grass on any stadium field we found would be an issue. That is why, for months I tried, unsuccessfully, to get an artificial turf field donated, an entirely frustrating exercise. I believed that one of the most wonderful gifts any company could give to the people of Tanzania would be a turf field, which would be playable year 'round, regardless of rain, drought or use.

Every grass field I ever saw in the country was wholly dependent upon rain, which comes and goes with the season. What a noteworthy thing it would have been if some company, most of which were earning good profits from their growth by installing turf fields in America, might have had the vision and global sensitivity to donate a field in Tanzania! Regrettably this didn't happen, not this time around.

We were clearly going to have to find the best of the worst and work with it. So there we were on the hunt for grass in northern Tanzania. To find grass, Frank and Dr. Meyer had both mentioned the possibility of moving the game about fifty miles (eighty kilometers) west from Moshi to Arusha. I figured it couldn't hurt to take a look.

Arusha was larger and much busier than Moshi, and appeared to be the northern Tanzania epicenter for activity, business, and politics. Arusha was also the regional hub for tourism, and understandably so, the safaris and mountain climbs leaving from Arusha are numerous. Mt. Kilimanjaro was just to the east and three National Parks including Tarangire National Park, Lake Manyara National Park and Serengeti National Park lay to the west, as well as the Ngorongoro Conservation Area nestled between Arusha and the Serengeti.

Ultimately, our search for grass wasn't as difficult as I thought it would be. The first stadium Frank took me to in Arusha was the Sheikh Amri Abeid Memorial Stadium, home of the Arusha FC (the Arusha soccer club). This was a historic stadium, the site where the Tanzanian National Flag was first flown in 1961, after gaining their independence from Great Britain. The very first thing I noticed when we walked into the stadium was the grass, long, thick, green grass. I was thrilled! The location couldn't have been better, right in the middle of the city, where hundreds of people meandered by the entrance daily. During our visit to the stadium there were even people inside milling about on the track and in the stands. The field, while satisfying our need for grass, had seen better days, and still wasn't perfect by any means. It was an older stadium for sure, with concrete stands all around the stadium and a small covered area on the west side closest to the street, with seating space for about 1,500 spectators. The stands sat a short ways back from the field, due to the cinder track encircling it. But there was grass, along with installed soccer goals and, as with seemingly everything in Tanzania, a lot of signs advertising beer, sodas and mobile phones. Certainly it would still take a lot of work to make it look good for game day, but at least there was grass. I quickly told Frank, "We have to find a way to play here."

Because this was pretty late in the event planning process, press releases had already been published saying that the game would be played in Moshi at the University Stadium. So upon my return stateside, I made a call to Chris and Sandy and told them, "Hey, a little change in the plan, we need to change stadiums and cities for the game."

"What?"

"Trust me, it's got grass, it's in a bigger city, the city has better hotels, it's got more people…this is the place to do it."

As with most things, Chris and Sandy decided to trust me on this one. Thinking back over the phone call as Chris recalls it, "What were we going to say? I mean Patrick was there; he checked it out and was seeing everything in person. I had never been to Africa. Playing in Arusha wasn't the original plan, but I trusted Patrick."

Now that is the kind of working partner we all seek!

Truthfully, I hadn't originally really hunted for the perfect stadium like I usually do when taking teams to a new country. The only reason I was set on Moshi was because that was where we were going to do the community service work with Del Christensen and his crew, and I just thought it would make life easier.

The lesson I learned through that experience was to take leads from other people, but also to check things out myself, and make my own decisions. Moving the Kili Bowl game to Arusha turned out to be a great call, another time God's hand was clearly in play.

Now that we knew for certain we would use the Sheikh Amri Abeid Memorial Stadium in Arusha, we still had to do a lot of preparation work for game day. In the months preceding the Kili Bowl, soccer would be played on the field, and I was a bit nervous about what condition the field would be in by the time my event rolled around. The stadium management, the CCM (Chama Cha Mapinduzi) political party, agreed to keep people off the grounds as of May 1, about three and a half weeks before game day, something I told them was critical. I also asked them not to mow it, just to let the grass grow and to seed the bare spots in front of each goal and in the middle of the field until I arrived, a week ahead of the game.

May quickly rolled around, and we were on schedule. My customary practice, prior to a new event, is to arrive a week or so prior to ensure that everything is in order. I flew into Arusha on Friday, eight days before our game. As soon as I landed I headed over to the stadium and was delighted to see the grass was nice and thick, nine to twelve inches high in some places. I loved it! In the previously barren spots there was a man with a hose watering the field, as well as a woman with a watering can, which resembled the old rusted metal cans my mother used to use when I was growing up. She was walking around, filling up the can with water from the man's hose and heading to the areas out of the hose's reach to water the grass shoots. I was amazed. I decided it was now time to mow the grass.

The next thing I knew, a smiling lanky man, about six feet tall wearing high rubber boots, showed up with a nineteen-inch Bowie push lawn mower indicating that he would mow the field. So he began to mow. And mow. And mow. It took him all of about four days to mow the entire field, working on a quarter of the field at a time and stopping three to four times a day to hand sharpen the blade on his mower. I would check in on him every morning and there he was working diligently, always with a smile on his face, to get the grass cut. By Tuesday afternoon he had completed his work. He asked me what I thought.

"It looks much better," I told him, still excited by the fact that we actually had grass, "but could you mow it one more time before the game?"

I felt bad asking him to do this as he had just spent four full days working, but the field still looked as though the lawn mower blade had never been sharpened, with clumps of tall grass sticking up here and there. He never complained, he merely smiled at me and said, "Okay, sir," and proceeded to start mowing the field again. The process was much more efficient the second time around, only taking two days to complete. I have to say, though, seeing these workers water and mow for days on end, without objection, to satisfy our need for a suitable field, was an astonishing act of patience and perseverance. I gained an even deeper appreciation of the Tanzanian's work ethic.

Knowing that I would be extremely busy working out last minute details of the trip before, and while the teams were arriving, I put my good friend John Roslien (JR) in the role of Stadium Manager. JR is a Certified Athletic Trainer and runs the Athletic Training department at Central College, an NCAA Division III college in Pella, Iowa. The entry sign to the town of Pella boldly reads, "If you ain't Dutch, you ain't much."

Love the attitude.

JR had developed a course of study, a major in Athletic Training, and each year he had about twenty-four students in his classes. In addition, we had worked together for over fifteen years, particularly on my events in Mexico. I knew I could trust him with this colossal task of transforming the stadium into something that our teams could be proud of, and where the coaches would be satisfied to play.

My Team Global staff, including JR, always arrives a few days before an event to get situated and do whatever prep work needs to be done, as well as to learn the ins and outs of the event. JR believes, "These are really critical days because we scout things out. We tour all of the facilities we are going to use, we get familiar with the hotels, where we are going to eat, where there are stores. We learn the basic things so when we get coaches, players, parents, and friends and family asking us in the lobby, 'Where do we get an American paper?' or, 'Where is it safe to get a cup of coffee?' we are able to answer all of those questions."

I took JR over to the stadium when he arrived on the Tuesday night before Saturday game day, to show him the field, explain what my plans were, and what I needed him to accomplish in order to get the field prepared in time for Saturday's game. A bit overwhelmed possibly, but ready to take on the challenge, he simply stated, "What time to we get started?" From 8:30 the next morning when I dropped him off at the field, till around 7:00 p.m. that night, and for the next three days, JR and his helpers worked busily on field preparation. They worked hard to turn a mangy soccer stadium into a football stadium with lines, goal posts, down markers, flowers, and entranceways.

Muhammad, the key guy who managed the stadium, spoke decent English, and was pretty much the only person JR could communicate with all day, as his helpers didn't speak any English at all. Needless to say, there was a lot of pointing and drawing of pictures to communicate. JR is amazing at his level of communication without having any idea of the language. He displays that talent each December in Mexico and did so here in Arusha as well.

During the day, in the midst of stadium preparation, the national Track and Field team showed up for training. It was interesting to see these premier athletes, with the best of the best in apparel and equipment, running on a dirt-poor stadium cinder track with a bunch of locals standing, watching, and cheering them on while they trained. All the while JR and his crew were moving ahead with our field transformation.

Prior to traveling to Tanzania, in order to transport all the items in the most cost effective way, I sent boxes of all sorts of game field equipment to each member of my staff for them to pack in their checked bags. I had sent JR the twelve orange pylons that outline the end zones. When they arrived at JR's house in Iowa, he pulled one of them out and realized it weighed at least twenty pounds as it had a solid piece of steel rod in it to hold it upright. He later shared that he had thought, "I am not going to carry over 200 pounds' worth of football equipment to Tanzania." So before he left he cut the big metal rod out of each and left them at home. The pylons were only one-fifth of the weight they were originally, so altogether they weighed just over 40 pounds versus the original 200 plus pounds. Nobody knew the difference. The end zones looked official.

While JR was busy with the field preparation, TAHA (Tanzania Horticulture Association) was also in the stadium making it look presentable with truckloads of flowers, bushes, and trees. The field and the stadium itself looked pretty plain, actually run down, so back in March I reached an agreement with TAHA to decorate around the outside of the field and to create an entrance way for the teams to run onto the field. In return, I provided them with an array of sponsor benefits.

Since Tanzania's inception into the Floriculture Industry in 1989, Tanzania has become a major player in this multibilliondollar trade, particularly in regards to the export of cut roses and chrysanthemums. The industry is especially profitable in Northern Tanzania around Mount Kilimanjaro, Moshi and Arusha, where the favorable soil, climate and proximity to main roads and international airports allow for the best growing conditions and easy access to trade. TAHA provides technical support, market analysis and political advocacy services to this sector of the Tanzanian economy to help develop and further expand the industry.

With some direction from JR and me, the individuals from TAHA worked diligently all day Friday and Saturday morning, sprucing up the field and stadium. One lady seemed to take very special care and interest to insure that each flower, bush and tree was properly situated. She was a tall, attractive, slender girl in her mid twenties, very pleasant in demeanor. When I mentioned to her that she was doing an impressive job, she almost seemed embarrassed. I do love it when people take pride in their jobs simply for the sake of doing a good job. Her name rang with a wonderful Tanzanian sound, Naiga, and she and Sandy Clubb became fast friends.

The TAHA volunteers situated dozens of potted palm trees and other bushes and plants with height around the perimeter, about ten yards off the sidelines. This helped give the area surrounding the field a little charm. Then, in the covered grandstands they carefully arranged bunting along the railings. On the front rails they added wound strands of flowers, mostly roses, to make it especially colorful. They draped the VIP area with brilliant hanging flowers. Finally, following my rough drawings, they created the archway for the players to run through, onto the field, I thought it would be a good backdrop for photos. They proceeded to build it right in the stadium, having brought metal and twisted wire with them with which to construct the arch. JR told me that it took them seven hours to get the archway the way they wanted it, but that seems to be the way it was with every element of this event.

Because it was the first time this type of game had been staged in Arusha, everything had to be created from scratch.

When the workers painstakingly got the metal structure in place, they finished it off with hundreds and hundreds of long stem roses of every color, woven into one another. The entire scene was splendid and created a beautiful layout, and an inviting atmosphere.

The other structures we needed to go around the field sidelines, amidst the plants, were for the banners and signage representing the companies and sponsors we had worked with on this event. I had ordered A-frames from a local businessman as well as the banners that would be attached to them. The business owner had them all ready for JR when he arrived at the field. There were banners representing Younger Optics, TAHA, and TANAPA. We also had banners for the Cultural Heritage Center in Arusha and the two main hotels we used, Kibo Palace and The Arusha Hotel. To top it off we had a couple of Global Football banners. As it all came together, the stadium was looking more and more like an American Football Stadium, with 14,000-foot Mount Meru standing guard to the north.

While the playing field itself had been the main focus, the final major obstacle was the two sets of goal posts, which ended up being an issue of their own. I had sent a diagram to Muhammad months before, specifying the size measurements for NCAA goal posts, asking him to have the local folks weld posts out of round pipe and to please have them ready when we arrived, with the soccer goals already removed. I thought everything from there on should be relatively easy.

Around midafternoon as JR was setting up the stadium, the goal posts arrived. Before installing them, the crew first had to remedy the fact that the length of the field was not long enough for the 120 yards needed per NCAA guidelines, including the two ten-yard field zones. To resolve this issue, they put down about two feet of sand from the end of the grass onto the cinder part of the track. We still didn't quite get the field to the required length, so, for the entire length of the field they proceeded to make each yard space about two inches shorter than what they should have been. Adjust, with poise! No problem, this happens all the time when we convert soccer fields into football fields. It might not be quite regulation, but I can tell you that no coach or player or official or fan missed those two inches.

Now that the field was properly measured and lined, it was ready for the goal posts. We knew that the football goal posts weren't going to end up where the soccer goals were, and new holes would have to be dug for the uprights at both ends. The newly constructed goal posts themselves looked good, especially considering this was certainly the first set of American football goal posts ever to be manufactured in Tanzania. They didn't look perfectly square, but they would work. While the field was being lined and extended, a separate crew was carefully painting the goal posts. They would apply a coat of bright yellow paint, take a break, come back and paint some more. When the time came to put the goal posts in the ground, about five members of the stadium crew, including JR, tried their best to place the goal posts into the holes that had been dug by hand; but without any success, despite using thick ropes and adding numerous bodies. Seeing as they had welded the goal posts together using heavy four-inch steel pipe (I had suggested three-inch), and made the uprights about ten meters longer than they had to be (like rugby), the posts were impossibly heavy to lift with the manpower at hand. They continued to try with ropes and ladders. They even had dozens of men come in off the street to help, but they just couldn't lift it up high enough to get the post to drop in the holes. At this point, after nearly an hour of struggling, it was time to take a break and rethink this dilemma.

Muhammad called a friend who worked at a dump nearby. A short time later his buddy showed up driving a huge frontend loader. I'm not sure how far he drove this massive piece of machinery, but it barely fit through the entrance into the stadium. The scoop of the loader still had gunk in it, the tires reeked of garbage, and the men could hardly stand to be close to it. The innovative workers then struggled to jerry-rig the goal post to the scoop bucket and helped to straighten the unwieldy structure with their ropes and ladders, while the front end loader lifted it…a liability nightmare…but they got it into the appropriate holes, centered it and filled the holes with cement as if the process had been no big deal. The same successful process was then repeated at the other end of the field. When the goal posts were finally up, they looked absolutely beautiful against the late afternoon deepening blue sky with Mount Meru hovering in the background.

Other small pieces of stadium preparation we managed to get constructed, brought in, improved or upgraded, included the scoreboard, which consisted of a big hunk of metal with a space for numbered cards to be hung; much like the kind of scoreboard you might see at a little league park some three decades ago. A young Dutch man, Andre De Beer, who proved to be extraordinarily helpful in gathering children for the clinics and halftime show on game day, had some of his school kids put the scoreboard together. The older students then were the ones who kept score during the game the next day.

JR's other task (he is never done) included serving as the public address announcer and disc jockey for the game. In order to get this set up, he had brought each of the national anthems (Star Spangled Banner, Tanzanian, and Mexican) with him from Pella, on an iPad he borrowed from his daughter. On top of that, he had a whole assortment of other songs that he played throughout the game, from the time the whistle blew for a dead ball to the time they snapped the ball for the next play. However, getting the iPad hooked up was a bit of an ordeal. Electrical connections in Tanzania are different from those in America, so he had to get a store to make a converter for his iPad so that it would function properly. On one of his first days there, JR made friends with two Tanzanian men who, after he explained what he was looking for, led him all over town until he found a store that would build him the proper converter. Thankfully he thought ahead as that process ended up taking a half day in itself.

For the PA system, a group of local people came into the stadium on Friday and brought all of the microphones, speakers, and other equipment needed, as the stadium wasn't wired for sound as one might expect. They did a great job setting it all up, almost too good as it was unbelievably loud for anybody sitting in front of the speakers.

JR's job as the announcer during the game ended up being quite entertaining for him and relatively easy since 90 percent of the fans in the stadium didn't understand American football, nor did they understand much English. This is when JR can truly shine, when nobody knows what he is saying!

Therefore, he didn't really have to announce play by play all the action. The only challenge was that we didn't have a visible game clock, which everybody could have seen. Throughout the entire game, you could hear the various coaches asking the onfield officials for the time. This was just one of the small challenges of playing internationally, where you don't always have the comforts of home.

Throughout the final set up day on Friday, Tanzanian locals would come off the street and wander curiously into the stadium. They would point, look around, and engage in a few words, not quite sure what was being constructed on their field. There were only a couple of kids who stuck around all day, sitting off to the side, smoking weed. Muhammad explained to JR, regarding one of the kids, "This guy's crazy, but he is not dangerous." I guess that's as opposed to the guys who are crazy *and* dangerous! It was clear that everybody was intrigued with the whole project. There were a couple hundred Americans in town, so it was obvious that something different was going on. This curiosity probably helped with attendance on Saturday though, as the entire city wanted to see what this sport was all about.

In the end, game day setup worked splendidly and as JR recalls, "It was just an amazing thing, how this all came together. The average fan from Iowa or Tanzania who walked in the next day would never understand what it took to get that place ready for them to play. The goal post story was one of the funniest situations I had ever seen on a Patrick/Global Football trip." With the great work of JR, Muhammad, and the rest of the crew, we were ready for an exciting matchup between the CONADEIP All-Stars and Drake University!

View from the Summit

I learned early in my business that delegating was an important piece of the puzzle. My events are too big for me not to entrust duties to my team members. If I want a job done well, I can't rely upon doing it all by myself, I have to give the task to somebody I know will do it well, and likely even better than I could have done it. That is why I have a team I can trust, and one that is made up of individuals with a variety of skills. It is truly everybody working together that successfully connects each piece of the event. That is why I take the people I do. I know them and can trust them to do the job to the best of their ability, which makes for outstanding events.

9

If It Were Easy, Everyone Would Do It

Oftentimes we feel like we are in control of our lives, but in reality it is truly God's plan that we follow; and what a beautiful plan it can be!

Local child at football clinic

The planning for this trip started long before CONADEIP had signed on to join in the event in July 2010. It began in Coach Creighton's mind before he even approached me, as he had a pretty clear vision of what the primary components of this tour/ event would be. He also had a keen perception that if this were to be successful, in large part it would be guided by the hand of God. Chris' staunch belief in this, as well as that of Sandy Hatfield, was an essential element that kept me focused and motivated during the trying times of the overall organizational process. I concurred on each of the key trip components, as they made so much sense. Therefore, Coach Creighton, Sandy and I were the primary driving force for the trip overview and all the details. As things progressed there was, of course, valuable input by others, especially Enrique and Frank Mella, as they had also taken the overall project on as their own dream!

We decided early on that the trip would be split into three main components:

1. Football
2. Community Service Work
3. Mount Kilimanjaro

While each of these were critical, it was agreed that the service work would be the most important, most lasting piece.

Within the football component, we needed to have a couple days of practice in Tanzania before the game so both teams could acclimate and prepare for this historic match-up. It also made sense to play the game early in the trip and culminate the entire event with climbing Mount Kilimanjaro, as the hike would most likely take all the players' energy. The climb would also serve as the emotional highlight of the event. From the very beginning, it was the service that truly motivated Chris, to have his student athletes do something for others less fortunate that would make a lasting impact on those who would receive the assistance, and those who would make the effort to help.

When I sat back and thought about what I was preparing to do, it was somewhat daunting. I mean, we were about to take a group of college kids, football players, from America's heartland, Iowa, and from Mexico, to Tanzania, Africa!

Two-thirds of these students had never been on an airplane; about one-third of them had never been out of their state. In Iowa, these were typically middle-class young men who would never have dreamed of getting up close and personal with an elephant in the Serengeti. In Mexico, some of the students were from fairly well off families, but many of them came from middle- or lower-class backgrounds. It is a long way from Monterrey, Mexico, and Des Moines, Iowa, to Tanzania, Africa.

Talk about a team building exercise. This was to be the epitome of team building, and then some.

Was it scary on my part to put this together? Not in terms of getting it organized; that doesn't scare or overwhelm me. I realize it is simply a step-by-step process regardless of where in the world I am putting together an event. Sure, this one was a bit more 'out there', and because it was the first time it had ever been done in Africa I figured the process might take a bit more effort and creativity. Ya think?

The only fear I had was that the event wouldn't actually occur, that something beyond my control would prevent it from happening. With all of the world's turmoil, with all the funds needing to be raised, with all the uncertainties of airlines, and with it being in Africa, it seemed almost anything could jump up and stop us. When the teams departed their homelands it had been just three weeks since our nation had finally disposed of Osama bin Laden, so there was clearly a state of high alert worldwide, expecting some sort of retaliation from his radical followers.

Finally, there I was, on the still, warm early evening of May 19, 2011, on the tarmac apron of the quaint Kilimanjaro Airport awaiting the arrival of two American football college teams from two different countries halfway around the world. When the lights of the KLM jumbo jet appeared like an apparition over the jungle to the north I realized that indeed this was about to happen, that what so many had planned and worked on for nearly two years was going to become a reality.

Suddenly, my Texas-based AT&T mobile phone rang, startling me, as I had not heard it make a sound for days. You see, to call out of or into Tanzania from the USA cost me about $4 per minute, starting at the moment the number was dialed! So, upon waking each morning, I would check my messages, emails, voicemails, and texts, then turn the phone off by noon when people in America would be starting their days, so as to diminish my potential costs. I did have a Tanzanian mobile which I wore out during my stay there, as it worked wonderfully and only cost about 2 cents per minute to use.

On that particular night, I had kept my American phone on just in case a worried parent or family member called to inquire about their son winging his way to Africa. When the phone rang, I noticed the 515 Iowa area code so I decided it might be important and answered. A pleasant, professional sounding lady introduced herself as the assistant to Dr. Maxwell, President at Drake, and wondered if he were available to speak. I told her the KLM jet was just coming to a halt and that he would be visible soon, but that it might take a bit to unload the entire group of passengers. I suggested that perhaps I give him a message and have him call back soon. She said that would be fine, and then went on to provide me with a chilling statement regarding security, which instantly sobered my giddy mood.

Security is a concern on all of my trips, but Tanzania was different. Tanzania is a democratic country that had been quite stable and free of many of the military and terrorist problems that have plagued other African nations. One only need look at a map to see that Somalia and its rebels lie close by to the northeast. Being post-9/11 and with Osama Bin Laden having been taken out by our SEALs not even a month prior to the trip, there were obviously concerns we had discussed with the local military. The fact that this was going to be a fairly visible international sporting event and tour, with worldwide publicity, we were not just going to slip into the country unnoticed, play a game, do some service work, enjoy a safari, and climb Africa's tallest peak.

During the week leading up to the teams' arrival, I met with the regional Chief of Police, a large gregarious man by the name of George (I never learned his last name). He was most anxious to get our detailed itinerary, which I happily provided him. He indicated that he would ensure our safety while in his region which included Arusha, Moshi, and Kilimanjaro. In fact, during the entire trip we were attended to by a convoy of some eight Jeeps with four armed guards per vehicle, along with three canvas-topped personnel trucks each with sixteen armed men, so I sensed they truly meant to keep us safe. And I was *okay* with that. In fact, that group escorted our entourage of fourteen twenty-four-passenger mini-buses wherever we traveled. It sure made getting across town much faster and simpler as the traffic on Arusha's main east-west road was on the verge of mayhem all hours of the day.

That being said, the phone call I received from Dr. Maxwell's assistant still made me a bit nervous as she proceeded to leave her message for Dr. Maxwell. She related that she had just received a call from the State Department in Washington indicating that their people in Tanzania had picked up some "chatter" among Somali groups, discussing the Drake visit to Tanzania. She had been told that there was no imminent threat nor were any direct threats made, and that for now the trip should go on as planned. However, they did want to make Dr. Maxwell aware of the situation, and that my core group of leaders—Sandy, Coach Creighton, Enrique and Dr. Maxwell—should at least discuss the realities now unfolding.

Wow! It would be terrible if, after all this work by so many people in so many places, we would have to completely alter our plans and cancel the trip and just turn around and go home! Of course, the only thing worse than that would be if, in fact, an attack were to be made against our remarkable group of young men, university staff and families.

Fortunately, nothing ever came of this and only a few of us ever even knew about the "chatter." Interestingly, the day before the game in Arusha Stadium while I was checking on JR and his crews' progress busily preparing for the game, two American men sporting Ray Bans and grey suits, white shirts and ties came walking in. It was obvious they weren't just average Joes walking in off the street to take a peek at our decorating skills. I went over and asked them if I could help, and they responded that they were from the American Embassy, doing a security check as the US Ambassador to Tanzania, as well as the Mexican Ambassador to East Africa, along with a few other national dignitaries would be in attendance. So I gave them the printed game day itinerary, pointed out where our VIPs would be sitting, and went over some of the stadium logistics. They said they were going to help add to our attendance on Saturday, explaining they would have about five hundred security, or, as they called them, "plain-clothed people," in the crowd. I was extremely pleased to hear we were being looked after so diligently.

Both teams departed the western hemisphere on a Tuesday; Drake by air from Des Moines, Iowa, while the Mexico team bussed overnight from Monterey and arrived in Houston where they began their flights. They drove across the deserts of Northern Mexico at night to avoid the possible dangerous activities with various cartels and narcotic trafficking on the roads there, which have, unfortunately, become all too prevalent. In Houston, just as in Des Moines, I had arranged for the CONADEIP travelers to pack eight deflated footballs per individual into their bags before walking into the airport. I only wish I had personally witnessed that chaotic scene curbside when my friend met them in his minIván packed with footballs!

Then off they went. One group from Houston, the other from Iowa, destined for an adventure they had dreamed about, we had planned for, one we all knew would alter the lives of each participant in so many ways.

The teams arrived at the Kilimanjaro International Airport, which consists of one long runway, a one-story small terminal building, and adjacent parking lot with no lights, around 8:00 p.m. on Wednesday evening. Surely this group from middle America and Mexico had some odd dreams in-flight. Now these 194 intrepid souls were in Africa, welcomed by a full orange moon to the east. They received an exceptional welcoming party outside the terminal as they exited the plane, with fragrant rose leis prepared by a handful of TAHA representatives and traditional Swahili dancers to help make their first moments in Tanzania memorable. The welcome was well received and appreciated by players and staff alike, who exclaimed, "We have been here for ten minutes and we love it already!"

I knew that they would step off that flight anxious about what the country would look like, how it would smell, and how they would be received. First appearances are so important to a group like this which had just traveled for hours and hours, so I wanted to make it special. When it comes to hospitality, the Tanzanian people are at the top of my list. When people ask me what are the people of Tanzania like, I comment that they display the hospitality of the Latin Americans, the work ethic of the Japanese, and the friendliness of Americans, with each of these carried to the furthest extreme.

After an hour and a half motor coach transfer along the dark, tree-lined road to Arusha, the weary travelers were eager to check into their hotels. I was quite pleased with what we were able to find for accommodations, especially in Arusha, which was critical as those were our game preparation days. The city of Arusha boasts a number of four-star hotels, each with its own unique style and history. After investigating six to eight potential facilities on my previous trips, we settled on The Arusha Hotel and the nearby Kibo Palace. I found those hotels to be ideal for our situation as they were both happy to reserve a sufficient number of rooms and were ideally situated about a quarter mile from one another, making communication and transportation easier.

Mexico stayed at the relatively new Kibo Palace Hotel, a clean, stylishly African facility with a tall tower of rooms and large dining areas both inside and out by the pool patio area. In contrast, we housed Drake at the historical Arusha Hotel, along with my Team Global staff. Though up to date and considered today as one of the leading hotels in the region, The Arusha Hotel was first built in 1894 and claims to be the oldest quality hotel in East Africa. It was a marvelous place with impeccable service, attentive staff, verdant gardens and a historical array of posters from when some of its many high profile customers, John Wayne and crew, stayed there for the filming of *Hatari*.

On their first full day in Tanzania, we started our visitors off with a spectacular full breakfast buffet at their individual hotels and then boarded the comfortable twenty-five-passenger coaster buses. With our police escort front, back and in the middle, the buses made the half-hour drive across town to the practice fields without incident. The drive in itself was fascinating, providing a snapshot into life in this northern Tanzanian city, which is the staging point for most safari and

Kilimanjaro expeditions. There was one major through street running east and west, which attracted every sort of motorized and nonmotorized vehicle. Our buses were among the largest and cleanest on the road, though we shared the potholed asphalt with an array of small sedans, mini-pickup trucks, and passenger vans known as dahli-dahlis, often jammed full with arms and heads sticking out of the windows. There were also passenger buses running between cities, and cargo trucks carrying anything and everything.

The sides of the roads provided a pathway for pedestrians of all ages, bicycles with one to three persons aboard, large wheelbarrows being pushed and carrying loads of iron, sand, food, cement blocks, and even large mirrors and windows. Just off the side of the road was a constant sensory overload of people offering goods and products from their shack-fronts, tire and auto repair shops, raw furniture stores, baskets of colorful food items, soda and candy vendors, etc. Everywhere we looked there was visual advertising for the various mobile phone companies as well as the local beers, bearing typically East African brands such as "Kilimanjaro," "Tusker," and "Serengeti Beer." Of course, as in all cities of the world, there was quite an array of men, women, and children just hanging out, watching the world go by, which on this rare day included a fleet of freshly-cleaned Coaster Buses full of Anglo and Hispanic people gazing and snapping photos.

The practice fields were located within the Tanzania Game Trackers facility (TGT), a sweeping, rural area owned by a Houston car dealer who I never got in contact with personally, though not from lack of effort. It was rumored to have the "best grass in East Africa," and I am not sure that they were wrong. The facility included a few lush and expansive soccer and rugby fields tucked in among hundreds of acres of lush coffee orchards. Far to the west the hills of the Rift escarpment rose to provide a splendid backdrop, offering a breathtaking location for the African sun to set each evening.

As it worked out, the best training fields were side by side, so the two teams practiced adjacent to one another. Neither coach had ever experienced practicing alongside a team they were about to play later in the week, but it worked out just fine. The teams had lunch and then proceeded to direct another African first, a youth American football clinic, under the leadership of Coach Creighton and Coach Maya.

Every coach I have had the pleasure of working with truly enjoys arranging and executing this type of event, having the chance to instruct youngsters in the basics of the game. In this case, with boys and girls who had no idea whatsoever about the sport, it would be especially challenging. In fact, throughout my travels in Tanzania I found it quite rare to encounter anyone who had even seen a photo or video of American football, it was a totally foreign concept to nearly all the locals. The coaches also saw this as part of the 'service projects,' since it would provide the Drake and Mexican student athletes the chance to work hand-in-hand with the local children, teaching a game our young travelers knew well.

On behalf of Global Football, leaders of Arusha Irie reached out to numerous public and private schools around Arusha, inviting the children to come and play. Andre De Beer, took on the challenge of contacting the various schools, after we met and discussed what I wanted to do with this clinic. Remarkably, he was able to attract some five hundred local children each of the two training days, dressed in their school uniforms, which often included skirts, sweaters, and leather shoes. They all came to enjoy and learn how to play American football. He was even able to arrange local buses to provide transport, as the TGT property is located outside the city to the west, limiting access otherwise.

The spirit of those instructing and those learning was contagious and inspiring! The scene with five hundred fresh Tanzanian faces catching, passing, running, jumping, laughing, cheering, and high-fiving was one of the most memorable of the entire tour, or of any I have helped organize around the world. We generally found the boys and girls to have large, long hands, which allowed for some talented receivers. They would gracefully "get some air," jumping at ease over obstacles or simply to go after a pass. And the girls with their long school uniform skirts never had a thought that they should not be playing this stereotypically male game.

While Coach Creighton and Coach Maya coordinated the clinic action, utilizing their players and staff, a Notre Dame friend of mine,

Reggie Brooks, joined in the fun. Reggie was an outstanding running back for the Irish in 1993-95, earning All-American honors and a Heisman Trophy candidate. His role at Notre Dame involves managing Monogram/Football and Alumni Relations, and I knew his personality would help motivate the young Tanzanians on the field. As would happen, one father with by far the largest teenage boy in attendance was eager to have Reggie work one-on-one with his boy. Watching a huge 15-year old work on his footwork with a legendary Notre Dame student athlete made me wonder even more broadly of the possible impact this day might have. Reggie was simply brilliant!

Another vividly memorable scene came upon arrival the first day, while the actual Drake and CONADEIP teams practiced, the dozen or so Drake parents on hand performed a much-needed task. You may recall that we brought along in everyone's checked bags about a thousand rubber footballs to use in the clinics and to then donate to those who attended. Well, before these could be used, they would have to be filled with air, so we broke out the small hand pumps I had packed, screwed needles on top of each and the men and women began the tedious process of pumping the balls up with African air. Fortunately, I had thought to include in my jammed baggage a large quantity of mesh bags in which to carry the inflated footballs. So as they were pumped up, the individual rubber footballs were placed into the mesh bags, and a huge pile was created, providing a cache for the youngsters. They were used extensively for the two days of clinics, then distributed to each child who attended the game and took part in the halftime fun, and now can likely be seen being kicked and passed all around Arusha. The experience was a lasting memory certainly for each of these youngsters.

Following the practice and youth clinic, some of those in our group headed out to visit and perform initial service work at various orphanages and schools in the area that Dr. Steve Meyer and his wife Dana had arranged, while others headed back to the hotels. These visits provided individually unique moments for each sub-group, and their stories would light up the evenings back at the hotel. Some recounted small private schools with open-air classrooms while others commented on the traditional Maasai village they had been invited to see. Still others helped feed babies in a hospital while some brought small gifts to children in a pre and post-operative medical center.

One day in Tanzania and already the lives of those who ventured there had been altered in many positive ways. That night, following dinner, one of the biggest student athletes from Iowa commented to me, "This trip has already been so worth all the effort it took to get here!"

The following day was very similar, but with more energy among all the travelers who had now had the pleasure of two full nights' sleep in comfortable beds, after their restless night in flight. Breakfast, practice, and lunch were followed by a large press conference on the steps of the clubhouse at TGT. National, regional, and local media from every form of broadcast and print were eager to learn firsthand what this American football sport looked like in person. They also were happy to gather information about Saturday's upcoming game, which they could then disseminate to their followers. Such a game had never been seen in all of Africa, ever, much less in Tanzania!

They listened eagerly as both coaches talked about their teams and their preparations for this trip and the upcoming game. They also learned from the Tanzanian Sports Council Chairman Colonel Iddi Kipingu, why he was so supportive of this event. He noted how South Africa had the past year become the worldwide host of soccer (referred to as *football* in most of the world), and that it was very special for Tanzania to host this historic American football event.

Just after the media festivities we hosted the second youth clinic for a separate group of about five hundred youngsters, which proved even more spirited than the previous day. This was due primarily to the fact that the student athletes and coaches now had some idea what to expect, and were also better rested.

After the clinic was finished we all went out to visit other orphanages and schools, and then returned back to the hotel for a hearty meal and team meetings in preparation for the Kili Bowl the next day. All of these athletes and coaches had performed this night-before-game ritual many, many times in their lives, at all levels of play. But this was unique, unknown, never before done on this continent!

On Saturday, May 22, 2011, the Global Kilimanjaro Bowl was finally here! The playing field looked beautiful with freshly cut grass, white lines and hash marks, potted plants, trees, and flowers surrounding the perimeter, compliments of the Tanzanian Agriculture and Horticulture Association. The rose archway was ideal for the teams to run through to enter the field, at the 50-yard line. It was classically Tanzanian, handmade, and beautiful yet built upon a simple foundation.

By the 1:00 p.m. kickoff, the bleachers, which ringed the entire field, and the VIP section seating shaded from the sun by a metal tin roof, were filled with nearly twelve thousand excited and intrigued viewers anxious to witness the first American football game in Africa. For most in attendance, this was to be the first American football game they had ever witnessed.

Among the spectators were the American Ambassador to Tanzania, Alfonso Lenhardt; Mexico's Ambassador to East Africa, of which Tanzania is a part, Luis Javier Campuzano; the host nation's Deputy Minister of Industry and Trade, Lazaro Nyalandu; and a procession of dignitaries.

Maasai tribesman and women entertained the crowds in lieu of the cheerleaders usually seen in American stadiums, rocking to the action and their own drumbeat as they saw fit. They were fully outfitted in their traditional clothing, with face paint, hand weapons, and drums.

In stark contrast to them was the television mobile production unit, whose electronics were somehow packed into a panel truck parked on the stadium cinder track in line with the goal line on the home side of the field. Connected to this truck were five cameras shooting the game, switched live by a director working his control board squeezed into the bed of the truck. They covered the action as best they knew, never having had the opportunity to actually watch and shoot this sport live and in person. They did a solid production job, but at times were fooled by play fakes, and seemed unsure when to follow whom. There was one cameraman, the "high center" shot which is so critical, who had to spend his afternoon perched thirty feet atop the VIP seating tin roof. His only access to the site was a step ladder he scaled before kickoff, as the tin often creaked and cracked under his weight, and the mid-eighty-degree sunshine had to feel like more than a hundred up there by the end of the game.

My own highly talented TV director/cameraman, Tim Brockman, with whom I had worked for some three decades, roamed the sidelines and captured the true emotions on the faces of the participants and fans, his vast experience enabling him to record some of the best on-field action.

Obviously, we did not have a talent pool of American football officials in Tanzania upon which to draw, so I had reached out to some men who had worked other international games and special events for me. As with what became the norm for most everything connected to the Kili Bowl, I found a wonderful group of eager, willing, and talented game officials who paid their own way to be a part of history in Africa, and in this sport. Led by longtime Big Ten referee Bill Lemonnier, the six-man crew traveled to Tanzania, prepared for the game with nightly meetings, attended practices and the youth clinic, visited some of the area sites and schools, and enjoyed a one-day safari. They then worked the game, which was not simple due to the competitiveness and totally different styles of play between Drake and CONADEIP. Adding to the international flavor of the event, these men came from Mexico and Poland as well as the USA.

While the stadium facilities might be considered "run down" by American standards, the Tanzanians' great pride in their country and belief in their independence remain strong. How special it was that the teams representing Drake University and the CONADEIP member universities of Mexico could stage this memorable contest in this stadium.

The game itself was exciting from the vantage point of those who understood what they were watching as well as those who didn't. From the moment the two teams ran out onto the field through the flowered arch the crowd was engaged, cheering for every action. Most moving was the Opening Ceremony where the temporary loudspeaker system installed especially for this game blared out the national anthems of Mexico, then the United States, and finally Tanzania. While the anthems took over ten minutes to complete, it provided plenty of time for all to gaze around at the scene, to take pride in being there, and to simply enjoy witnessing history being made. To me this moment is always a rush, listening to the national anthems, regardless of where the game is being played. Especially at this time and place how special it was to take a moment to give thanks for all our blessings, and for having the chance to be there, at that time and place, with those people, for that game. It was the most wonderful day to be in Arusha, Tanzania.

The first half saw the defenses dominate, which was no surprise as neither team had played an actual game in many months. The only first quarter score was a 27-yard field goal by Billy Janssen, giving Drake a 3–0 lead going into the second period. While there was constant action, numerous dynamic run and pass plays, as well as some big defensive hits that fired up the attentive crowd, it wasn't until the fourth quarter that points were scored again. It was hard to say which team was in control of the game, as both defenses were stubborn, not allowing either offense to mount any sustained drives.

The halftime show didn't involve the typical American style marching band and cheerleaders. Instead, we invited the one thousand children who had joined us in the clinics the previous two days to play some football on the stadium field. In gratitude for their halftime performance, Drake and CONADEIP parents and staff who traveled with us handed each of the children a football and Global Kilimanjaro Bowl t-shirt as the youngsters ran onto and around the field. It didn't matter much what the kids did while they were out there for their ten minutes, as I simply instructed them to "go play." It was one of the favorite halftime shows I have ever witnessed as a thousand children were center stage on this hand-built American football field, just having fun and laughing with one another as they tossed around their new footballs.

Both teams remained scoreless throughout the third quarter, but there was plenty of hard-hitting action, led by both attacking defenses, which energized the eager fans who made up for any lack of game knowledge with enthusiasm. At the start of the fourth quarter, CONADEIP running back, Edmundo Reyes plowed through the Bulldogs to score, putting them in a 7–3 lead following the extra point.

Soon after though, Drake answered with its own scoring drive capped off by a TD pass from Nick Ens to Joey Orlando, making the score 10–7 and getting the fans as fired up as they had been all day. Now they were totally engrossed in the on-field action, loving the big yardage plays and realizing the remaining game time must be running short.

CONADEIP came roaring right back, running Reyes up the middle and hitting play-action passes to the outside against a tiring Drake defense. Suddenly, Reyes burst up the middle on a perfectly executed draw play, gaining twenty-eight yards before tripping on his own move at the 5-yard line. If he didn't trip in the open field, he would have scored for sure. With their backs to Mount Meru, the Bulldogs' defense stiffened and would not allow the All-Stars from Mexico to score and take back the lead.

Instead, Drake took over on downs backed up against their own goal line. After grinding out a few first downs, they were forced to punt to CONADEIP, allowing the Mexicans one final chance to score and win the game. On first down, however, the Drake linebacker was able to strip the Mexican running back of the ball and recover the fumble. In the final minute, Drake's Patrick Cashmore scored with a power run up the middle for a touchdown with 2:03 remaining to give Drake a 17–7 lead.

The Kili Bowl was a dramatic win for Drake and as we would find out later in the year, just the start of their upcoming conference championship football season. While most of the fans in attendance didn't fully understand the specifics of the game, they were able to capture the passion of the players and the speed of the game. The experience left those in attendance intrigued by the sport that had just been played as an official game for the first time ever on the African continent. No matter what the future holds for the sport in Tanzania or Africa, there can never be another first game!

The contest was competitive to the final play, as the two international teams battled gallantly on the field. Within moments after the clock had expired, and hands were shaken, the rivalry was over. From that point on and throughout the rest of the trip, the two teams came together as allies who would proceed to work with one another, support one another, endure challenges together, share their talents and efforts, and experience an unknown world together.

View from the Summit

Having been on the sideline for hundreds of football games throughout my life, initially as a player, sometimes as a fan, and over the past nineteen years as an event producer, many of them tend to run together in my memory. Certain ones, however, stand out distinctly, for various reasons. The 1968 Prep vs McDowell clash in Erie, the 1971 Cotton Bowl vs Texas, 1997 Tazón Azteca in Toluca, 1998 Pop Warner game in Moscow, 2000 NFL Global Jr. Championship in Atlanta, 2009 Notre Dame Japan Bowl in the Tokyo Dome, the 2009 Vienna Charity Bowl featuring Illinois Wesleyan and Austria, 2012 Global Ireland Football Tournament, 2014 Penn State vs UCF in Dublin, Ireland each bring back a stirring memory.

None, however, comes close to the 2011 Global Kilimanjaro Bowl, for so many reasons.

10

Love Grows When People Serve

> Coming together is a beginning. Keeping together is progress. Working together is success.
>
> —Henry Ford

Not only did these individuals get to volunteer, they actually experienced the impact their work would have on the community. The village of Tema is about as close to a self-sustaining community as one can get, and for a single night, individuals from Drake were able to walk in their shoes. They were able to experience the strength of community and family, the hardship of living off the land, and the love of perfect strangers who took them in and shared everything important in their lives.

Drake player during community service

Game over! That single moment, the most historical element of the tour, was completed. Now it was time for what we all thought would truly be the most lasting and significant component.

While the excitement of the game was still upon us, everybody had to switch gears and prepare themselves quickly for the activities yet to come. The next step on our journey in Tanzania was for the two teams to come together and perform community service work in and around the area of Moshi, a much smaller town than Arusha located about two hours east, sitting directly south of Mount Kilimanjaro. In Tanzania, the idea of community service is not quite as foreign a concept as it is in many other African countries, or even throughout the world, but it still isn't as widely accepted as it is here in the United States. Del Christensen of IRIS was able to clarify: "The mentality across most of Africa is that if I am going to do all this work why shouldn't I get paid for it? So the idea of volunteering is not something they jump at, but they do band together as a community in the Tanzanian villages to accomplish common goals."

The morning after the game and football awards banquet staged in the garden area of The Arusha Hotel, everybody packed their gear for the next nine days of community service, safari and climbing Mt. Kilimanjaro. To make life easier, we had everyone leave a duffel bag with their football gear behind in their Arusha hotels. Other bags and buses packed, we headed off on our ride east towards Moshi. On the way we passed the road south that would take us back to the JRO Airport nine days later. With clear skies off to the northeast, for the first time we all saw the striking façade of Mount Kilimanjaro in the distance, looming more than 19,000 feet in elevation, towering above the surrounding savannah. While it was my fourth trip to Tanzania in the past year, this was only the second time I was able to catch a full glimpse of the majestic mountain's summit as clouds usually block the view.

When we finally arrived in the bustling town of Moshi the group split into four different hotels, all within walking distance of one another, as no single hotel had the capacity of those we had secured in Arusha. After settling everyone into their respective rooms, we immediately began to prepare the groups for their first afternoon of service work, organized by Del Christensen of IRIS (Iowa Resource for International Service).

Originally known as the International Center for Community Journalism, IRIS is a nonprofit organization founded in the early nineties by the former Governor of Iowa, Bob Anderson. At the start, its focus was teaching journalists, primarily from former Soviet states, the role that a free and independent media can play in American democracies. One has to keep in mind that this was not long after the end of the Cold War, and the role journalists played was tremendous in that transformation. It wasn't until 1996 that the International Center for Community Journalism changed its name to Iowa Resource for International Service, expanding its mission to other peace building program work.

Their early programs were almost entirely for adults, where they would bring men and women from other countries to Iowa for specific education programs. In 2010, for example, a group from Belarus came to learn journalism techniques, as well as a group from Turkmenistan that took courses on renewable energy. They have also recently had women leadership groups from sub- Saharan Africa come to learn the role women can play in a democratic society, and in particular in elected politics.

Since the 2000s, though, IRIS has delved further into youth programs including the YES (Youth Exchange and Study) program. YES is a scholarship program created by the US Department of State's Bureau of Educational and Cultural Affairs. Through this program, students are brought to the United States for a year to attend school while they live with a volunteer host family and engage in volunteer service. They also participate in other activities to gain a deeper understanding of American society, and acquire leadership skills, all while helping to educate Americans about their own culture. While one of the primary goals of this program is to expel myths about other cultures, it also focuses on teaching the students about community service in the hopes that they will start their own community projects back in their home countries.

IRIS's YES program focuses primarily on the Saharan Africa region including Nigeria and Tanzania, bringing to America high school juniors ranging in age from fifteen to eighteen. Throughout their ten months in the United States, the students are expected to complete at least two hours of community service each month for a total of twenty hours. Many students surpass the required hours; some even perform over one hundred hours monthly during their stay. The idea of having the students focus some of their time on community service helps them to see how much volunteer work can impact a community. The program alumni will then hopefully take their enthusiasm back to their home country with them. Unfortunately, this is where they tend to hit a brick wall, as many ideas may not be as readily transferable to their country. IRIS then continues to coach these students, allowing them to realize that they don't necessarily have to do something BIG, that even a little progress is still progress. Many of them then take larger project ideas from the US and scale them down in size for something feasible in their situation.

One example Del gave was a student from Arusha who liked the idea of Library Book Mobiles. "If people can't come to the library, take the books to them," she explained. "She wanted to help schools and students get more access to books. The tricky part was that while she loved the concept, she had to figure out how to do that in the Maasai culture. So she created a book basket program where she would put a dozen books into a basket on her bike, and then she would ride from one school to another.

At each stop, she dropped off a dozen books and picked up the dozen she had dropped off the week prior, taking them to the next school. With just her bicycle, basket and strong will she created her own bookmobile."

A few years prior to the Kili Bowl, Sandy and her family became a host family to a high school student from Nigeria, which is where her relationship with IRIS began. Hence, when we had discussed doing community service as a portion of the trip, Sandy was able to contact IRIS and eventually set up our Tanzanian projects through them.

Del Christensen, the Executive Director of IRIS, Ms. Grace Foya, the Tanzania Director, along with IRIS's Moshi associate, Mrs. Mary

Minja, worked closely with Coach Creighton to manage the coordination of the athletes for the different volunteer projects and funding for each. For the most part, the ideas for the projects came from the various YES alumni students in Moshi and the surrounding Kili area.

The goal for the projects was to have the US and Mexican students work together. Because of the sizes of their respective squads, this usually turned out to be three Drake players and two CONADEIP players, with IRIS's YES exchange student alumni mixed in and taking the lead on each project. Overall, we wanted to combine being able to accomplish a number of volunteer projects with a lot of manpower while also making sure that the alumni students were in the forefront of the activity. As Del explained, including and involving the YES alumni was crucial, stating, "Long after the Drake and CONADEIP teams leave the communities, our alumni students will continue building all kinds of street credentials because they were seen as the ones who brought the football players over to volunteer in the community. My goal was to push as much of the credit for the volunteer work to the alumni so they could use that street cred to continue future efforts within the community. That will help them to do many more valuable things within their own communities for years after."

The volunteer projects undertaken by our teams were highly varied, both in the size and type of project. For the most part, the thirteen different volunteer groups we created did their work over a period of three days. At the end of each day they retired to their hotels for dinner and sleep. These volunteer opportunities gave the athletes, coaches, and everyone else involved a chance to spend time working side by side with the local residents, to learn what life was really like in Tanzania. It also provided a chance to see firsthand how many of the Tanzanians lived day to day. Sadly, these days millions are without much of a family primarily due to the ravages of HIV.

This entire trip to Tanzania helped reinforce how important teamwork was in all aspects of life, not just on the football field. Dr. Tom Westbrook, who continued to teach his course while on tour, recalled one of the projects where a group of volunteers, himself included, built a volleyball court for a local girls' school/ orphanage. The volleyball court was to be made out of concrete. So while some of those in our group were helping to clear the area, others worked to mix the cement. It quickly became apparent that there would not be enough cement to complete the court. Fortunately, not three hundred yards away was a quarry of old, discarded bricks. The group figured the easiest thing to do was to walk to the quarry, carry the bricks back and proceed to smash them to use as fill, a very long and tedious process. All of the sudden a bunch of the young Muslim schoolgirls, dressed in their uniforms with lily-white shawls, lined themselves up from the quarry all the way back to the volleyball court. "Like a fire brigade, the girls passed the bricks down the line to the football players whose time now wasn't spent lugging two to three bricks at a time back and forth, but instead were busily smashing the bricks given to them by the school girls," Dr. Westbrook exclaimed. "It was a beautiful site to see." Throughout the process not one person complained, they all were simply happy to have been involved in the project as now they would have a stake in the success of their own school.

As the boys, girls and adults worked together in harmony the silence was suddenly broken, stirred up with screams and children running. Somebody had pulled a brick out of the quarry and uncovered a snake. Quickly one of the workers appeared with a machete and chopped it up before it could do any harm. Needless to say, everybody got right back to work, albeit while treading a bit more lightly around the quarry!

Not only did the volunteer work help to unite the student athletes with the local Tanzanians, it also brought the American and Mexican players together. The very same players who had competed against one another in a very contentious game on the football field just a few days earlier, were now on the same teams. Each working towards a common good, all rivalries were left behind, and now they were best buddies focused on a more important goal.

During one project, in particular, it was obvious that close relationships had developed. A field was being cleared in a pretty bad part of town. As Dr. Westbrook recalled, "It was probably the poorest area I had ever seen in my life." While at the field, a local soccer team came over to watch the volunteers complete their work. Right after their work was completed, the Mexicans and Americans came together in their heavy work boots and dirty clothes to form a team and play in a friendly game of soccer against the local Tanzanians. Watching the student athletes playing soccer together, you would have thought they were playing a championship FIFA match, given how hard they were playing. It was a highly spirited contest, as the American/Mexican team lost by one goal against the local team. Dr. Westbrook explained how this game allowed the Mexican and American athletes to be participants, and also observers. By participating in that pick-up game of soccer, they were also able to observe a group of Tanzanian youth athletes, firsthand, in the midst of poverty, having the time of their lives playing sport. "You can't write in a journal the impact of that; you can't write it in a paper, and you can't quantify or qualify how powerful something like that is, but that is what these trips do. They open your mind to things that you read about, things you might even be tested about, however, until you see it and experience it, you don't fully understand it."

The original thought about volunteer activity housing was to have the volunteer groups stay with host families instead of in Moshi hotels. While people like Del, Sandy, and Coach Creighton were in favor of this idea as they felt it would be the experience of a lifetime, not everybody was comfortable with it. The athletes' questions were numerous because they couldn't seem to get past their fear of the unknown.

What kind of village would they be in? Would there be toilets? Would they have to boil their water? Would the food be safe? What if they were kidnapped? What kind of wild animals would they come in contact with?

As Del explained, "It is those kinds of misconceptions that require the experience of staying with a host family to really change one's mind. It's the same way in the other direction. It takes a Tanzanian student coming to Iowa, experiencing winters and feeling freezing temperatures and walking on the frozen river to thoroughly understand that…wow… you don't die if you get cast into what they would consider a refrigerator."

Another thought was to have athletes spend their evening meal with host families in Moshi. We believed this would give the boys an opportunity to experience local life, at least for a couple hours per day.

Unfortunately, the Moshi Police put the kibosh on that the first day, stating that they did not want the groups splitting up and going into unsafe areas of town alone at night. We felt it was best to go along with the legal authorities to keep everybody safe.

Ultimately only one group of thirteen individuals ended up staying with host families in a remote village known as Tema, in the rugged foothills of Kilimanjaro. The group only stayed one night, but it was recounted as one of the most powerful experiences of their lives, and a decision they will never regret. While the overnight trip to Tema was designed for the student athletes, many of them were nervous about the ordeal and choose not to go. Instead, the group of thirteen included only a few student athletes who were accompanied by one of the coaches and Sandy, her husband Chris, and their two children, as well as her father and two family friends.

The Tema group's experience didn't start at the volunteer site, but rather began the moment they crammed into the minIván and headed on their way to the village. The road was not very well traveled, with slippery red mud that the van slid and got stuck in on multiple occasions. Fortunately, the football players who joined the group included a couple of linemen who could pick up the van and move it back onto the road. Eventually, however, the vehicle got stuck for the very last time, which is when the group's hike to the village started. Not long into their hike they came across numerous people from Tema who were waiting for them at the bend in the road. The community members were dressed in their native headdresses, carried drums and other instruments that they played as they escorted the volunteers up the rest of the hill to the village school. The area felt overwhelming as Sandy described, "Wherever we looked there were these enormous waterfalls, it was just absolutely breathtaking. You could also see for hundreds and hundreds of miles into and past the foothills of Kili onto the savannah."

As a welcoming, the villagers performed a ceremonial dance which involved grabbing their visitors' hands and bringing them into the throbbing action to share in their welcoming and excitement. As night quickly fell upon the village the ceremony ended and the locals brought their guests refreshing soda to savor, which to the locals was a delicacy of sorts as it wasn't easily accessible. It was then determined that each family would take one volunteer into their home, with the exception of Sandy and her husband, each of whom brought one of their young children with them. The families waited patiently while the headmaster sorted out who went to which home. One by one, he called up the volunteers and pointed with whom they were housing for the night.

Sandy and her nine-year-old daughter, Skyler, were placed with George's family, a wonderful small man who spoke but two English words during her whole time with him, "Must hurry." The second they were matched up George took her by the hand and off they went into the jungle, hurrying to utilize the little light that remained. They hiked for what felt like two miles, almost straight up the mountain, holding onto vines to help them along the climb. Almost to the house, a little girl met them, taking Skyler with her further into the jungle. Finally at the house they walked inside what they believed was the kitchen, a small room with a mud floor, ceiling, a wall and two cows and a calf who announced their presence with loud moos. The house was small, but George, his wife, their eight children, their nephew and his mother all lived there together peacefully. George had Sandy and Skyler sit in the living room as he brought his children in and introduced them. Sandy tried to communicate with them with little success, so she asked her daughter to take out her drawing pad and a pen. Skyler proceeded to draw a picture for them which she passed to the children. One of the little boys reciprocated by drawing another picture, and before you knew it all of the children came to sit around Sandy and Skyler, drawing pictures and trying to teach them Swahili. In a matter of ten minutes, the young Iowan knew how to say her numbers in Swahili!

Each volunteer had their own unique experience that night in Tema, likely to stay in their memories forever. In the morning the volunteers were brought back into the village center where they started to build a foundation for a new schoolroom. Lunch that day was fresh chicken that the locals brought over alive, killed, and cooked over the fire pit near where they were working.

Tema was an interesting village to work in as it was very community-oriented and even had a "community day" of sorts where each member of the community, whose day it was to volunteer, must participate in the project of that day. If a member did not show up some of the locals would go to their home and make sure that they were sick or seriously injured to the point where they could not help, or else that member would have to pay for not showing up by giving the rest of the community something of value, like a chicken or goat. As it turned out all of the locals who worked that day were in charge of walking down the hill to the quarry and carrying rocks up for Sandy's group to use in laying the foundation.

At the end of the work day, with the sun diving behind Kilimanjaro, the group from Tema drove back to Moshi to join the rest of the volunteers, sharing stories the entire drive.

As a follow-up to the Moshi area visit and work, Del Christensen offered a recap of what was accomplished through all the volunteer efforts with IRIS.

At the end of the three days of work by about 180 total visitors, the athletes, coaches, staff and parents had accomplished the following:

- built two new classrooms
- built one orphanage dormitory with twelve rooms to house ninety-six children
- repaired and painted classrooms in four schools
- constructed four different recreational facilities (soccer, netball, volleyball and basketball)
- planted more than five hundred trees
- Nearly thirty alumni and selected YES students from around the country traveled to Moshi to participate in the volunteer project component of the Kili Bowl!

On top of all the work our travelers did with the IRIS projects, one group of Drake players was sent off separately to the nearby village of M'Buguni on a STEMM project with Dr. Steve Meyer and his ten-year-old son, Josh. Apparently, one night shortly before we made our initial contact in Iowa, Steve was putting his son to bed when Josh turned over to his father and told him that he had something he wanted to talk to him about. As a parent Steve was a little worried, thinking there might be trouble at school. Instead, Josh went on to tell his father, "This isn't going to happen any time soon dad, but someday you are going to die."

Somewhat taken aback by this comment, Steve asked his son what he was getting at. He went on, "When you die, who is going to do your mission work?" Now this is a child who had grown up seeing his parents travel to Tanzania almost every six months of his life. He knew all about their work in Tanzania but had never joined them on any of their trips to date. Josh went on to explain to his father that he had been thinking about this for a while and that he had decided he would give up his anticipated pro football career to become a doctor and go to Tanzania to continue in his father's footsteps.

At that point, Steve told his ten year old, "Son, you have just won yourself a trip to Tanzania."

Steve's point was simple, if his son was going to take over as the STEMM mission director, he should go to Tanzania and see firsthand what he would be doing. His boy replied that if he was going to go, he wanted to do something.

The timing was perfect. The Kili Bowl was going to be the next summer; this would be an ideal time for Josh to make his first trip to Tanzania. Josh proceeded to come up with his own community service project to be done while he was in Tanzania, calling his campaign "Small Change for a Big Change." Through asking people via the local media to donate their spare pocket change, he was able to raise $5,500!

Using the money he raised and by working together with a group of Drake football players in Tanzania, Josh and his helpers were able to build ten new chalkboards for the STEMM orphanage, as well as build a chicken coop. The chicken coop, which looked nicer than most of the houses the locals lived in, was built to provide the children with a solid, sustainable source of protein from the eggs. Josh's first trip ended up being the trip of a lifetime and one that the children of M'Buguni will forever be grateful for.

View from the Summit

It is amazing what can be accomplished when you bring people from a variety of cultures and backgrounds together for a common goal. The original purpose of our trip was to play a historic game of football, but it became so much more than that. The second the game ended the two teams divorced what happened on the field and formed one team. They worked hard together, they laughed together, and they even pulled pranks on one another.

It was obvious that the community service work they were doing turned into more than a duty. As each of the football players worked with one another and experienced firsthand the daily lives of the locals they were helping, something changed inside of them. They were able to look outside of themselves and see what a difference an individual can make in the world. As Mother Theresa once said, "Love grows when people serve."

11

Safari—Lions, Leopards, And Ticks...Oh My!

ATTENTION PLEASE—DO NOT TAKE liberty with wild animals as they are dangerous and always remember that whatever you do in the park is at your own risk.
—Park Management Sign,
photographed by Drake player

How many people have gotten to watch an international soccer game in the middle of the Serengeti together with Africans, Mexicans and Americans alike? Not many, and I am proud to have been one of them!
—Dr. Enrique Ramos

On safari, Ngorongoro Crater

Over one million tourists flock to Tanzania every year to experience its amazing array of premier National Parks and Conservation Areas. With a quarter of this country's land set aside for conservation purposes these areas host an abundance of flora and fauna, much of which is endemic to Tanzania. Within these parks, Tanzania can also boast having Africa's highest point, Mt. Kilimanjaro, as well as Lake Tanganyika, Africa's deepest lake.

Since this is one of the most bio-diverse countries in Africa, it would have been a shame to spend time in Tanzania without enjoying a safari through its magnificent ecosystems. Even though our trip was packed with activities, allowing very little time for kicked-back leisure, we did manage to fit in at least one day of safari for each person on the tour. During the three days devoted to community service, we split the group of climbers who would later hike Mt. Kilimanjaro into thirds. Each day, Frank Mella's staff took a group of travelers on a day trip to Tarangire National Park, located about four hours southwest of Moshi. Due to the abundance of water provided year round by the Tarangire River a wide variety of animals can be found in this preserve, including many of the migratory species such as antelope, elephants, lions and leopards. While not as well known as the Serengeti wildebeest (Western White-bearded) migration, a different race of wildebeest (Eastern White-bearded) make their way through Tarangire every year, arriving in the park during the dry season (the United States summer months). Although these students were only able to enjoy a one-day safari, it was a unique outdoor experience that most, admittedly, would never get to do again.

The morning after the three days of community service were completed, everybody packed up again and loaded their bags with what was needed for the next six days, the final stage of the trip. The rest of their gear was left behind in the hotels to be picked up on the way to the airport. For most of our contingent, the last six days would involve the monumental challenge of hiking toward the peak of Mt. Kilimanjaro and back down.

Understandably, and mostly due to medical reasons, not everyone on the trip desired or was physically able to make the climb. The nonhikers were taken by our local staff, led by the main safari guide, David Awed, on a six-day adventure through four of Tanzania's most renowned protected areas: Lake Manyara, Tarangire, Ngorongoro and the Serengeti. Not a bad alternative!

For many the prospect of not being able to climb Mount Kilimanjaro with their friends and teammates was a huge disappointment, especially for those who were prepared to hike until they received minor injuries while playing in the football game just days earlier. For others, like Jennie Phillips, who had to make the difficult decision of choosing between the hike and the safari, it was about having the opportunity to see and enjoy something she would never get to witness in the United States. While she knew it was possible to hike a mountain in the US, she would never be able to watch these types of animals in their natural habitat, and that became her deciding factor.

Just one day into the safari any disappointment that individuals may have felt about not going on the hike quickly disappeared as they witnessed life in the wilds of Africa, up close and personal.

In many respects, the safari offered the staff and players a whole new appreciation for the world outside of their own. As Dr. Westbrook explained, the safari provided each person an opportunity to see and understand things that they would most likely never get a chance to experience again. It also allowed the students to learn about animal behavior and their own specific roles in the environment.

As David noted, while the group gathered above a tepid waterhole, "In a pool full of hippos surrounded by hyenas, if the hyenas ventured into the pool they would easily be destroyed by the hippos, most likely torn to bits. But, if there is a sick or dead hippo in the pool, somehow the hyenas and hippos have an unspoken agreement that the hyenas can go in, remove that carcass, and they won't be touched. So you begin to understand that there is a whole other world, this animal world, which functions totally separate from humans."

The first day of their safari the group arose before dawn and drove to Tarangire National Park. Along the route, they encountered a small number of Maasai herding their cattle on the barren soil just as their ancestors had done in the Great Rift Valley of Tanzania and Kenya for thousands of years. Children who looked to be four to eight years of age were seen carrying sticks, helping to herd the cattle, doing their part for the tribe. The adults, dressed in their traditional bright red clothing and multi-colored beads, allowed the tourists passing by to take photos in exchange for some coins. Jennie had brought the leftover pin-on Kili Bowl buttons with her which she gladly gave out to anyone they passed along the way, mostly the Maasai. Children loved them and would mob around her for more. Further along the road they passed local people carrying colorful plastic buckets to and from the well site, or the nearest pond or stream, to access their families' only fresh water for the day.

Finally into the park, everyone enjoyed their first sighting of elephants not fifty feet away from the vehicles. They also saw herds of plains zebra, gazelles and giraffes wandering about, grazing lazily on the sparse grass. After a wondrous day of driving and sightseeing the group arrived at camp. As Jennie noted, "When we turned the corner into the campsite, we pretty much had no idea what to expect. We hoped for the best and prepared for the worst, but didn't even know what the worst was. Then it really hit me, oh my gosh, this is how we are going to live for the next five days!"

For the sake of comfort, throughout the Tanzanian parks, there are luxury lodges that many tourists opt to stay in. Our group, however, did not stay in the lap of luxury as they were on a true outdoor safari journey. There were campsites throughout each park with a covered pavilion providing an area under which to eat meals; as well as rustic (sometimes smelly and not so clean) showers and toilets within walking distance of the tents. Every day a vehicle with members of Frank's crew drove out ahead of the group, where they set up each tent and cooked the meals. At night, while the group was sleeping, his crew also took turns standing lookout for any dangerous creatures that might be attempted to make off with an easy meal, since the camps were out in the open plains, without fences or walls for protection. In the morning, the crew efficiently prepared a hearty breakfast, and after the group left they would strike camp and head to the new site to start all over. The food was quite good and varied, always with something satisfying to enjoy, even for the nonadventurous eater.

The reality of the first night was a bit daunting. Everyone's senses were heightened, and their imaginations greatly expanded, especially those who hadn't had much prior camping experience. This was Africa, not Iowa or Nuevo Leon, and nobody knew what might be lurking just outside the camp's perimeter. The main worry as they all went to bed that night was the unnerving thought that the wild animals they had seen throughout the day, as well as other nocturnal critters, could be right outside their door at any moment, and in the morning. Or that a herd of elephants could become spooked and trample them in the middle of the night. Didn't happen.

Throughout their time together on safari it was actually the little things that created a close bond among the campers. For example, the first night one of the Drake players was paranoid about bugs crawling on him. Of course, when the others discovered this they got a hearty laugh out of it and when he attempted to rest they would use grass to tickle the back of his neck just to get a reaction out of him. It was hilarious.

What really struck each person was the sheer number of stars visible at night. Being so far from the city lights, out in open wilds of Africa, the night sky was unbelievable, filled with millions of bright, shining stars that one never even knew existed. Spectacular!

The second day the group packed up and headed to the Ngorongoro Conservation Area. The world's largest unflooded and unbroken caldera in the world, Ngorongoro Crater is home to some 25,000 large animals and the most comprehensive evidence of human evolution, spanning over the past four million years. In order to keep some sense of order and to be able to account for the volume of visitors each year, every vehicle had to register upon entering the park, a custom in all government managed lands in Tanzania. While stopped at the entrance of Ngorongoro, there were a number of signs warning tourists of the monkeys climbing around. Not that they were dangerous, just that they would just steal anything left out in the vehicles—cameras, phones, sunglasses, food… anything!

The group spent their second night camped above the massive crater looking down two hundred feet into the microcosm of African wildlife inside the 100-square-mile range within the crater. It was relatively cold on the edge of the crater, and wild hogs were abundant. The guides were extremely careful and reminded everybody not to bring food into the tents, as the hogs' keen sense of smell would likely cause an unwelcome visitor inside, disrupting sleep at the very least. The students learned a valuable lesson that night, early in the trip, and thankfully without any harmful consequences. Some brought snacks into the tents thinking it wouldn't make *that* much of a difference, and were awakened by the snorting and shuffling of hogs outside their tents at 3:00 a.m. The reality that these massive hogs could indeed smell the food, and easily rip through the thin tent wall to gain access, did manage to frighten the students. From then on they were extremely careful about following the guides' instructions. Good idea!

It wasn't always the large creatures that cause concern though.

There were many other creepy-crawlies that one might find disconcerting when out in the African bush country. Jennie was most terrified of these small creatures that she couldn't necessarily see crawling around her.

After they arrived at camp that evening, the ladies decided it would be smart to get their showers first to insure they would have hot water. So they dropped their bags outside of their tents and made it to the showers (they later came to find out that there were other, better showers just a little further off). Feeling clean and refreshed and wearing layers of clothing because they were at relatively high altitude, and the night air was chilly, the group sat around relaxing and chatting. All of the sudden Jennie felt something small crawling on her body. It was a tick! Ah, those demons of the wild, as Jennie considered them to be. Hurriedly, she grabbed my daughter, Xela, and ran to the bathrooms to do a tick check. Having grown up camping often in Texas and New Mexico, ticks were not an issue with Xela, but she wanted to be a good "tent-mate" to Jennie, so she obliged the search. They easily removed the singular problem bug, but because they had left their bags outside of the tent while showering they realized anything could have gotten into their clothes, and ultimately onto their bodies. They decided to do a complete clothing check to make sure no more ticks were present. For the remainder of the safari,

Xela gladly maintained a sense of calm, and great humor inside the ladies' tent. She applied her years of experience outdoors with our family camping trips and felt totally comfortable in this environment. Xela also embodies the most wonderful sense of ease, able to defuse most any tense situation, so her presence with the entire safari group was most welcomed.

Inside the crater the next day the safari group witnessed a wide array of animals including wildebeest clashing their horns, fighting one another, as if they were auditioning for a National Geographic program. One of the highlights of the day was seeing both a male and a female lion sitting alongside the road some seven feet from the vehicle, appearing quite exhausted. It seemed as though the travelers could just reach out and touch them. The guides explained that this was the end of the mating season, and the lions were too tired to move away from the vehicles.

Not much further up the road the group spotted one of only seventeen Black Rhinoceros who live in Ngorongoro. Black Rhinos are easily one of the most endangered large animals in Africa, with 90 percent fewer black rhinos in Africa than just four decades ago, due to relentless hunting and habitat destruction. While its future seems bleak, with conservation efforts there is hope that Black Rhinos will still be around for the next generation to enjoy.

In the evening, as everybody settled into their tents, many of the adults got together for an African-style happy hour, savoring the taste of warm beer they had picked up before the safari, along with a sip of tequila brought by Enrique from Guadalajara, Mexico. That night in Ngorngoro the group fell asleep to the gnawing sound of zebras munching on the grass directly behind their tents. When needing to visit the restroom at night everyone knew the herd of zebra was right behind the tents and wondered what predator might be lurking around waiting for its midnight snack. Needless to say, one didn't always make it all the way to the restroom, as a nearby tree would often suffice.

They awoke enthusiastically first thing the next morning, and it was off to the oldest and most legendary National Park in Tanzania, the Serengeti. The name means "Endless Plains," derived from the

Maasai language which reflects the true nature of the region. By this time the group had seen large quantities of zebras, elephants, giraffe and antelope, and strange to say, these were nearly becoming commonplace. Their hopes were now set on possibly spotting the rare cheetah or leopard. Welcoming them near the entrance to the Serengeti were a dozen lions lying casually in the open plains, simply doing what, for the most part, lions tend to pass their days doing, hanging out.

Further into the park, David was the first to spy a cheetah, only about twenty feet off the road. It was easy to understand from the cheetah's sleek body and long legs that it was made for speed. After capturing gorgeous images of yet another one of Africa's endangered animals, the group jokingly insisted on seeing a leopard, as if ordering a burger at a drive-in.

This was their lucky day because not fifteen minutes later David quietly pointed out a sleek leopard in the distance, sitting underneath a broad acacia tree. The amazed adventure seekers sat mesmerized for about an hour, just watching as the leopard sought protection from scavengers, climbing sleekly up onto one of the limbs of the tree carrying its freshly killed gazelle dinner with her, licking the blood off her mouth as she sank into her meal. Fortunately, our videographer, Tim Brockman, was able to capture the entire scene on his camera.

Everyone was completely awed by this extraordinary encounter. While it made sense that the leopard would run down the unsuspecting gazelle, capturing its prey, then stealthily haul the carcass up a tree to safely dine, the timing that enabled our folks to witness this exact moment was too special to be considered just good luck.

All over the Serengeti, there were scatterings of Maasai villages with dozens of stick huts and the people just going about their daily business of herding cattle. In general, the children and women tend to the chores of herding cattle, gathering water and preparing food while the adult men are rather sedentary. Quite a striking contrast between our everyday lives in most of America and Mexico. For the Maasai, their whole existence centers on survival and herding their cattle. They aren't looking to fill up every moment of their day with who to have coffee or dinner with, or how to plan their weekend. It was refreshing to see life how it used to be for all of us centuries back, revolving around life's rudimentary basics.

It was getting toward evening, and all were making their way back to the campsite when one of the vehicles got a flat tire. A flat tire is never fun for travelers anywhere, but often it is no more than just a nuisance. For those relying on that vehicle in the Serengeti that late afternoon it was rather frightening, as they had to stand outside the vehicle, directly next to the tall grass alongside the bumpy dirt road, and wonder if anything was waiting for them on the other side, just as night was settling in. Thankfully the driver, David, was extremely skilled at changing flats and did so efficiently, allowing the group to pile back into the vehicle and return to camp, seemingly just ahead of the attacking wild African beast.

That night the group dreamily watched the sun set over the Serengeti, waking up early in the morning to watch it rise again. All through the night instead of zebras, this time they heard water buffalo chomping their food and were finally lulled to sleep by the sound of roaring lions in the distance. Africa was becoming nearly normal, and comfortable, in its own way.

The group's first stop the next day was at a pool of stagnant water overcrowded with hippos and crocodiles. Amazingly, the two don't often attack one another. Hippos, while herbivores, can kill a crocodile if provoked. On the other hand, an adult crocodile can and will kill a hippo calf if the opportunity presents itself. Our visitors, though, did not get any such displays of rivalry between these otherwise calm creatures while on their trip.

The last day on safari was spent in Lake Manyara National Park, a tropical paradise in comparison to the dry dustiness of the Serengeti. Lake Manyara is connected to Tarangire through a wildlife corridor, which has proven to play a crucial role in allowing animals to migrate in a protected manner between the two parks, and is why visitors see many similar animals in the two parks. While teeming with all sorts of animals, Lake Manyara is best known for its baboons, Vervet monkeys, and Blue monkeys which hang playfully from the low-hanging tree limbs as the safari vehicles pass through. The group's last night was spent in a small clearing cut out from the jungle around the picturesque lake with monkeys constantly jumping around in the trees above them making all kinds of racket, as monkeys will do.

After six glorious days and five memorable nights in the wilds of Africa, these twenty wanderers were happy to get back to civilization where warm showers and clean beds awaited their arrival.

Upon returning to Arusha and slipping back into their comfort zone with hot running water, shelter, restaurants and people, the safari group reminisced on their week in the wild. Stories were shared about the boys who were afraid to go into their tents at night because of the lions they heard in the distance, about Jennie and how she wouldn't look up at the rafters to see the fist-sized spiders hanging above as they ate their meal, about the animals, the stars, the practical jokes…reminiscing about their entire trip.

One particular night on their trip boldly emerged as the most memorable. During their stay in the Serengeti everyone appreciated the fact that they were out in the wild with no apparent civilization for hundreds of miles. As everyone was setting up for camp that evening a conversation about an important soccer match that was on television that night in many parts of the world ensued. It was to be a highly anticipated match between the world renowned FC Barcelona and the infamous Manchester United Football Club, whose roster included a young, yet already famous Mexican by the name of Javier Hernández Balcázar, or *Chicarito* ("Little Pea"), as he was often referred to. Jokingly, the group asked the driver if they could watch the game that night, knowing that it would be a next to impossible task. The driver responded, "Oh, let me see what I can do." While surprised by his reply, the group was skeptical and went on with their routine tasks. After all, this was the Serengeti in the wilds of western Tanzania, on the continent of Africa, not Mexico, or America, or even Europe.

Around eight o'clock at night, while everybody relaxed with only the ubiquitous sounds of nature around them, the safari driver showed up and announced, "Okay, I have got a match." Everybody was a little confused. What did he mean? It was impossible! But they followed his lead and piled back into the Range Rover safari vehicles. After driving for about half an hour, the group arrived at a Serengeti Park Ranger Station. The rangers had set up a thirteen-inch black and white television in the corner of the room where about fifteen traditionally dressed Africans were sitting in plastic chairs watching the soccer game being played in far-off Europe between two of the world's greatest teams. The small traveling contingent of Americans and Mexicans joined the local group, all sitting together in the middle of the Serengeti watching FC Barcelona and Manchester United play for the title.

This was quite a unique mixture of fans to say the least. Whenever Manchester United marched, all of the Mexicans cheered, "Chicarito, Chicarito!" When Barcelona passed or scored, the Africans yelled "Messi, Messi, Messi," for their favorite Argentinean player, Lionel Messi. For the most part, the Americans were impartial, just enjoying the energy around them. At halftime they all enjoyed a locally brewed beer, Kilimanjaro brand, in the bar at the Ranger Station.

Enrique Ramos has often noted since that night, "How many people have gotten to watch an international soccer game in the middle of the Serengeti together with Africans, Mexicans and Americans alike? Not many, and I am proud to have been one of them!"

While the six-day, four-park safari was initially set up as an alternative to hiking Mount Kilimanjaro, it clearly became much more than that. Each person, whether they hailed from Mexico or America, came away from the excursion with a much greater appreciation for life in the wilds of Africa. Even though the camping experience may have been less than luxurious, and even frightening for some at times, it helped to bring the teammates, and those from two distinctly different cultures together in an especially intimate experience. They each got to know one other through these transformational few days far outside their normal comfort zone and by traveling in a rural environment with one another far from the football field.

For the student athletes, this experience would soon be translated to their teamwork during the season for they knew one another's strengths and weaknesses and worked as a team to succeed.

View from the Summit

It usually takes getting outside of one's comfort zone in order to embark on a truly memorable experience, something that may not be repeated but will certainly be remembered. When it is possible to share the experience with old friends and new acquaintances, it can be especially remarkable.

By its very nature life is full of disappointments; things out of our control. Each of the student athletes who journeyed on the six-day safari had thought he was going to climb Kilimanjaro, but then due to injury or illness had to change plans. Would any of them give back those days on safari?

12

Tupande Kileleni— Let's Climb to the Summit Together!

From the first time I heard this brief, poignant Swahili phrase I knew that it would be my mantra for the entire Global Kilimanjaro Bowl. As the event planning rolled along, evolving into the actual seventeen days in Tanzania shared with the 195 people who trusted me to insure it would all go smoothly, the overriding spirit of *Tupande Kileleni* was omnipresent. This saying, with its very clear meaning, Let's Climb to the Summit Together, got us up the mountain, and in fine style.

A commitment is a man's word, not so much to others, but rather to himself. Those who go back on their commitment, on their word to themselves, must forever live with the 'what if' that inevitably haunts them in moments of solitude.

Three countries summit, Mt. Kilimanjaro

While the group of twenty individuals headed out on safari, a couple dozen parents and wives headed back home to Iowa, returning to their newly revived blessed lives. The rest of the 135 student athletes and staff, including myself, rode somewhat pensively in our Coaster buses to the base of Mount Kilimanjaro to begin our six-day hike with the goal of reaching the summit of the world's tallest free-standing mountain!

Moshi's humid town air was full of excitement and anticipation as we hopped onto the vehicles for our drive from the comfortable hotels to Kilimanjaro, saying goodbye to civilization for a while. Due to the large number of hikers in our group we had decided long ago to split the two teams, having each group hike up a different side of the mountain, meet at the summit and climb down parallel routes. This was a difficult decision as we were so focused on doing everything together, but the hiking groups were large to manage as it was when divided in half.

CONADEIP climbed via the southwestern slope's scenic Machame route (also known as the Whiskey route due to its reputation for being a tough climb). Drake headed up the more remote Rongai route, the only access to Kili's upper reaches from the north. These distinctive trails, each unique in their daily challenges and vistas, but both starting at about the same elevation and, of course, ending at the same height, were suggested by Frank Mella. They turned out to be ideal for each group, different, yet so unique in their own way.

At the gate to the trails stood a sign that read "Points to Remember Before Climbing."

1. Hikers attempting to reach the summit should be physically fit. (Duh, these were all athletes; they should be fine…at least we would soon find out.)
2. If you have a sore throat, cold or breathing problems, do not go beyond 3,000 meters. (Everyone seemed healthy enough.)
3. Children under 10 years of age are not allowed. (Some rules are flexible and more like suggestions, right?)
4. If you have heart or lung problems do not attempt the mountain at all without consulting your doctor. (All good on that front.)

5. Allow plenty of time for the body to acclimatize by ascending slowly. (We were frequently reminded of this by our guides. Polé Polé…Slowly Slowly.)
6. Do not push yourself to go if your body is exhausted or if you have extreme. (Classically Tanzanian. Extreme what? This was something we focused on making sure each person was aware of.)
7. Drink 4 liters of fluid each day. Water is best, but fruit juices are a good supplement. (The guides helped make sure we stayed supplied with water and hydrated.)
8. If symptoms of mountain sickness or high altitude disease persist, please descend immediately and seek medical treatment. (We made certain that everybody was well aware of the dangers altitude could have on their bodies.)

Climbing Mount Kilimanjaro is actually one of the simplest high summit climbs one can attempt in terms of technique and actual equipment needed, but it is a massive challenge due to its elevation at 19,341 feet. No special gear such as ropes, crampons, axes or oxygen tanks is required. In addition, we had porters who carried the group's gear as well as our individual duffel bags and tents for us, a new way to climb for me, and a method I instantly appreciated. The only thing we had to worry about carrying was our daypack with water, rain gear, hat, gloves, sunscreen, camera and trail mix. Having hauled full backpacks of food, sleeping bag, tent, cooking gear and kitchen sink on numerous hikes throughout North and South America, the personal load I was asked to carry on Kili was a treat.

If climbing Kili was fairly simple, then why do statistics show that only about half of the people who attempt Mount Kilimanjaro actually reach the summit? To shed some light on the answer, George Mallory, a British mountaineer once said, "When I say that our sport is a hazardous one, I do not mean that when we climb mountains there is a large chance that we shall be killed but that we are surrounded by dangers that will kill us if we let them." While Kilimanjaro was not quite the

Mount Everest that Mallory was most likely referring to, his comments still apply to hikers everywhere in the world and not to be taken lightly.

The reason some 12,000 hikers who attempt to summit Kili annually fail to make it isn't because of laziness or not being strong enough to handle five to seven days of hiking. It is most often due to AMS, Acute Mountain Sickness, also known by many as Altitude Sickness. It is the result of the human body's response to a lower oxygen supply to the lungs and brain. AMS is no joke. One can be the most physically fit person in the world, yet not be able to make the ascent. AMS does not discriminate and if not careful it can be life threatening. The symptoms may begin with a simple headache, which most people shrug off as dehydration or exhaustion after days of climbing. But if not recognized and watched, it can quickly escalate to more serious, life threatening diseases including pulmonary edema (fluid in the lungs) and cerebral edema (swelling of the brain).

Knowing the seriousness of what we were about to undertake and the high probability of at least one, if not a few, of our climbers being afflicted with AMS, we were careful to take extra precautions. As divine providence would have it, one of the Drake parents knew a doctor by the name of Luanne Freer, who happens to be one of the world's foremost high altitude specialists. Dr. Freer worked for many years as a doctor in the Northern Rockies where she honed her high altitude medical knowledge and skills. In 1999 she took her first trip to Nepal and had since founded what is known as Everest ER, a nonprofit altitude emergency clinic at the base camp of Everest. Every year, from the first week of April till the end of May, she cares for four hundred to five hundred patients, over half of whom are the local Sherpas who had previously received little to no care.

Upon learning about Dr. Freer, Coach Creighton reached out to her inquiring if she would like to join us and serve as the official doctor on the climb, helping to make it as safe as possible for the team. She gladly accepted the offer. Dr. Freer joined a few of our planning conference calls in the months before flying to Tanzania, voicing her professional concerns about the high altitude risks all would undertake on Kilimanjaro. She also provided a very direct, thorough briefing for everyone the night before we all started climbing, which clearly stated the risks and ways to minimize them. For me, this also reinforced the severity of the undertaking we would begin the next morning, and my own personal responsibility for each of these individuals.

Throughout the six days on the mountain, both morning and night, she checked each and everyone's vital signs, among those in her hiking group, for symptoms of AMS. As it turned out, on the second to the last day of the hike, right at the moment when the two teams met up with one another at Gilman's Point, an hour from the peak, one of Drake's defensive tackles, John Sawhill, started showing the beginning symptoms of cerebral edema. Dr. Freer made it clear to both Coach Creighton and myself that John had to get down the mountain as quickly as possible as his condition was quickly worsening and could be fatal. We immediately took action and sent him down with one of the athletic trainers. Thankfully, he recovered quickly as he descended, but it weighed heavily on our minds for the rest of our time on the mountain.

When we initiated the climb at 7,200 feet elevation, altitude sickness was far from our mindsets, we were just excited and ready to tackle the mountain. I joined the Mexicans on the western slope as their group was a little smaller and they had fewer staff members joining them than Drake. Plus, my fluency in Spanish might come in handy in case of any emergency. My original plan was to hike between the two groups and try and spend half my time with each. While studying the topo maps more carefully the week prior to our climb I quickly realized this was completely unrealistic, so I stayed with CONADEIP the entire trip to the top. I had every reason to believe that my fiftynine- year-old body would be able to make this entire ascent to the summit, but was not sure I should push my limits by adding another 10 miles of hiking at that altitude in order to travel two days with Drake.

Before starting our trip, the Mexico team and I received an official sendoff and were given words of wisdom by Ezekiel Maige, Tanzania Minister of Natural Resources and Tourism: "If he makes it to the top, I know he has taken the advice of polé polé…that's slowly slowly. If you want to leave that advice, you may not. So I advise you that please go polé polé, that's slowly, slowly."

He didn't only say this as a key to avoiding altitude sickness, but also to keep us from getting too exhausted early on. It was a marathon, not a sprint.

On the northern slope, Coach Creighton gave his team similar words of encouragement. He was sure to impress upon his group the importance of teamwork throughout the next six days. We all soon found out that the physical strain of going up the mountain would not be the only obstacle to surmount. It was also incredibly difficult mentally and if you allowed your mind to drift toward negativity, there was no way you would make it to the top. Coach Creighton and I attribute most of our groups' success to the support provided steadily by their teamwork. The fact that these student athletes were already teammates and accustomed to encouraging and pushing one another to do their best, even in the most difficult situations, was what enabled so many to reach the top, thereby achieving their goal.

The first day's hike through the tropical forest was lush, verdant, damp and beautiful. We began mid-morning under a pretty steady rain, which evolved into more of a mist before settling into calm moist air with occasional drippings off the sagging tree leaves above. At this point, the trail was dotted by mud puddles here and there, and worn into nearly a two-lane dirt and mud track accommodating us to walk three abreast, and allowed for our porters to scurry by with their backs laden. Our focus was simply to walk, enjoy, breathe deeply, talk and dream. It seemed to me to be a relatively easy stroll through the woods, especially with the light weight of my daypack. About halfway through the day a group of Frank Mella's men quickly passed us, carrying massive piles of our camping supplies with them, food, fuel, tents, chairs, etc., wrapped in plastic tarps and bound by ropes. They forged ahead of us to set up camp and prepare our meal before we arrived. I couldn't help but notice their footwear, which ranged from simple rough leather sandals to worn running shoes to light hiking shoes.

If we knew nothing of teamwork before starting the climb that would change abruptly as we witnessed our mountain staff handle their roles individually and as a team. For our two climbing groups alone, Frank brought 511 employees with him. Split between our two groups were a total of 400 porters who carried all of our equipment including our tents, food, water, duffle bags with our change of clothes, folding chairs, propane tanks, stoves, large mess tents and anything else you could imagine one might need for camping.

What amazed me was that every day they traveled from campsite to campsite laden with bulky loads, constantly passing us while wearing the most basic footwear; and sometimes even going all the way down the mountain and back up to the new campsite in one day just to bring us fresh fruit and vegetables. They swept past us, always with a smile, a gentle greeting in Swahili, "Jambo," and then they were off.

There were seventy-two mountain guides who walked with us the whole way, splitting themselves up among the hikers of various speeds and always making sure that nobody was left behind. Then there were two lead guides, of which Frank was one. My team was led by a most dignified and confident young man likely in his mid-thirties, Amani Mtui. Their job was to set the pace, or have one of their other guides do that, not allowing anybody to pass them and to insure the group was on the correct route at all times. Most importantly, the lead guide had to keep track of those in the back of the lengthy row of hikers still moving forward, albeit at their own pace. At times he would be at the front, other times walking along mid-group, and often lingering to the back, only to move ahead once again. I swear the lead guides walked at least twice the kilometers we all did. It was obvious that all the guides took their jobs seriously, often asking how everyone was feeling, offering simple encouragement in their quiet, very chill Tanzanian manner.

Twenty-seven cooks accompanied us, providing delicious and hearty freshly cooked meals three times a day. Of course this also required the hauling of all this fresh food, huge cook stoves, large propane tanks and extra fuel.

To capture each and every moment of our climb were four photographers/videographers, each of them local Tanzanians we had sought out so that afterward we could edit a one-hour video show to air on CBS Sports Network. Tim Brockman was the show's overall director and lead cameraman, but with his one prosthetic leg figured it would be best for him to shoot the safari and allow others to handle the Kili trails. The cameramen also provided thousands of emotional still photos that we later turned into slide shows for each participant, focusing on their particular travel group. Personally, I did not know if I would ever be here again, so it only made sense to have professionals document the climb, for everyone's memory.

Finally, along the routes were six security officers from the National Parks Service who made sure our group was safe at all times.

These workers had their own specific tasks to perform, and they all worked together seamlessly to accomplish the common goal of taking care of each and every one of us as we made our way up the mountain. They worked extremely hard, assisting one another when needed, doing this with the utmost professionalism. It was an amazing ensemble comprised mostly of young men who had grown up in the region, many of them like Frank Mella, right in a village on the mountainside. This overall effort personified ultimate teamwork, which our coaches quickly noticed, and were happy to point out to their student athletes along the way.

Every night I would lie back in my tent, appreciative to hear the native Tanzanian workers laughing, singing and joking around with our climbers, bringing welcome joy to one another and to the entire camp.

At about 9,400 feet, that first night on the mountain was simply magnificent, our orange tents perfectly situated with a sweeping view of the sun glistening as it set against the ice and snowcapped steep façade of Kili's summit, still far up and in the distance. We had clear skies all around, a blessing we were provided with for most of the climb. Standing there looking at the massive ice field leading to the summit I envisioned what it was going to be like in just a couple more days, when I and over one hundred members of our team would be up there....on the top of Africa!

What a wonderful thought to drift off to sleep with, further coaxing my weary body into its deep slumber, as if any encouragement to sleep were needed.

The second morning I woke up to the sound of chatter in various languages all around the camp, Spanish, Swahili and English. As I was lying there snuggled against the fresh morning air in my tent and sleeping bag, one of the porters rapped on my tent door, called my name and delivered me a warm cup of mint tea, with a dollop of honey. That is what I call service!

A heavy dew covered the entire camp. Our tents were soaked, low hanging tree branches sagged under the weight of the moisture, and knee high bunch grass drenched our hiking boots as we headed to the large breakfast tent for morning eggs, toast, fruit, hot cocoa and avocado. Each of us had our own canvas folding chair in which to dine, seated alongside long plastic foldup tables jammed with all the condiments anyone might request in their hometown diner. "More coffee, tea, hot chocolate?" the helpers would gleefully inquire.

Before we began the day's hike, we were again reminded not to pass the head guide and to go slowly—polé polé. Seems on day 1 a number of players, along with a veteran mountain climber who was accustomed to being the leader rather than "one of the group," had charged ahead on their own, clearly breaking a hard and fast rule! There was a critical safety reason for this rule, and Amani made that understandable for all of us. After all, he, and ultimately I, was responsible for the safety of each individual and the group as a whole. A few of the heavier young men were talking about the previous day's difficulty, primarily due simply to the amount of pounds their bodies comprised, and that they had no option other than to lug every kilo along. The lighter, smallerframed teammates commented on how pleasant the previous day had been, noting that the altitude was not an issue...yet.

The first hour of our climb was pretty steep as we clambered over massive boulders through the grass and ever-shorter trees, steadily gaining altitude. At times, rolling clouds rushed up the canyon to our left, or west, enveloping us in a sweeping cloud cover which instantly burst open again into blue sky. Far ahead was a wall of rock running transverse to our route, looming as a barrier we would no doubt somehow have to cross later that day.

One of the many endearing traits of the Latin people, which I grew to appreciate decades ago when running backpacking tours in Guatemala, is their love of music, song and easy laughter. Our total hiking group of about sixty bodies spread out into subgroups along the trail, usually numbering some eight to ten each. At times songs would just ring out ahead or behind my particular sub-group, heartily sung by the Mexican boys, only to be joined in by the other groups of hikers ahead or behind. This Latin music, sung in Spanish and set against the backdrop of the boundless rocks and grasses, set a pleasant and happy tone to the entire scene. Nature, humans, mountain, song, Mexico, Africa—

Life doesn't suck!

While the morning trail was a bit steep, the route actually seemed to get easier as the day progressed. By midafternoon, we reached the unmistakable wall of rock, standing some one hundred feet above us. While it looked nearly impassable, our guides carefully led us up a step-by-step staircase-style trail cutting through the façade, up and over. Once on top the view to the north and east was vast and dramatically different from what had surrounded us all day. In every direction there were simply rocks, rocks and more rocks, strewn helter-skelter across the landscape. Through it a dirt path was worn, leading toward a smaller hillside of boulders just a couple of kilometers away. To the northeast the foreboding ice and rock wall that was the face of Mount Kilimanjaro dared anyone to attempt to summit from this side. Obviously, we would not attack Kili by that route as we were not prepared for technical climbing with ropes, crampons, carabiners, and all the tools needed. As we approached the camp I asked one of our guides what our route would be the next day. He simply replied, "We go around and then up. You will see."

I was happy.

By the end of that second day I was still feeling really good physically, but weary nonetheless, totally inspired to be on the side of such a massive piece of earth. There is a unique feeling that comes over a person's body while hiking, exerting oneself, especially in the wilderness, and even more so at altitude. While similar to the endorphin "high" runners and other endurance athletes report, this is different. It is fatigue most definitely, but overshadowed by a sense of accomplishment and rushing of blood to the recovering muscles, further enhanced by the spectacular vistas and memories of that day. One must experience it to truly understand, and everyone who has the strength within their body should definitely do so.

I can't say the same "outdoor rush" was there for everybody else as the group seemed to be slowing down a bit, feeling the wear and tear of two long days' hiking overall, and I could start to see signs of exhaustion. It was here that I felt it was mind over matter, spirit over pain, and attitude over inconvenience. I always feel it is my job to share this positive attitude while undertaking such a journey, so before dinner I ambled around the array of tents aligned across the barren field simply saying hello to all my teammates, encouraging them to take in the amazing views in every direction, inquiring how they enjoyed the ever-changing terrain, and reminded them of what they had already accomplished.

While wandering around I gazed far off to the west and noticed, jumping out of the low-drifting clouds, the perfectly conical shape of another mountain. This was in fact Mount Meru, situated just north of the city of Arusha where we had begun this tour and where we had been on game day less than a week ago. I swear this nearly 15,000-foot high mountain was not there when we arrived at camp about a half hour earlier. The clouds had simply settled down lower on the mountainsides, allowing us this majestic site. Again, I thought just how lucky I was to be there, with these people from three distinct cultures. I also wondered how my friends from Drake were doing on the opposite side of Kili, also making their way up to the top.

I would find out a few days later that they already had a coach and player feeling sick and feverish, not sure how much further they would make it. It felt very odd to have totally disconnected from them two days ago when we went our separate ways in Moshi, now heading up on different trails, living through similar yet differing moments in time, on the same massive piece of uplifted earth.

The third day I woke up, glanced out my tent door facing west, to the sun shining on the summit and eastern slope of Mount Meru, an active volcano. So striking.

The air outside was frigid, near freezing I estimated, making it rather unappealing to get out of the tent. In addition, my feet were feeling a bit sore from the two days' steadily uphill hike, and my legs a little stiff, but lean and strong from the effort thus far. What got me moving that morning was the anticipation of a delicious, warm breakfast awaiting me, and I didn't have to do any work to prepare it.

All around the campsite were hopeful white-necked ravens looking for an easy meal to snatch. At this point we were pretty high up, and the altitude was visibly starting to wear on some people. Breathing became a bit labored; talking was noticeably slowed, as was the hiking pace. I actually relish the feeling, perhaps oddly, but I find it enhances creativity of thought.

For Drake, the first of their members affected by the altitude was sent down the mountain on this third day. As we had been taught, altitude affects individuals in different ways at different times.

On the Machame route my merry band of Mexican amigos and I all headed off at our own independent paces, one step in front of another. The trail was marked by rock cairns every few hundred feet, noting possible wrong turns. We had now changed compass directions, going nearly due east across rolling terrain. In terms of getting up to the top of the mountain, we didn't gain much elevation on this day. It was more of a traverse across the side of the mountain and was used as an acclimatization day, a highly recommended key element to the eventual success of attaining our goal.

The primary plant life at this elevation was the Grand Sinecio tree, similar in shape to the Western Saguaro cactus; with a tall cylindrical shoot surrounded by leafy bunches along its lower parts. These were most prominent in the sides and bottoms of the canyons and ravines we would descend, traverse and ascend throughout the day's hike. Always the stark up-thrusted rock of Kili was to our left, massive and vertical, with ice in its crevasses and black rock shining. The day just seemed long, possibly as there was nothing new or startling to look at, and also knowing that we weren't accomplishing anything toward our ultimate goal of reaching the summit…or so it appeared.

While there was the occasional sunny spell, most of the day was spent in a cloudbank, which enveloped our hiking group, shrouding the walls of Kili, as well as the valleys far below. The day was highlighted by an all-out hot lunch served inside the meal tent, perched upon flat rocks on a windswept mesa. We had all expected just to stop briefly along the way, to meet some of the porters who would have our sandwiches and fruit, which had been the fare the first two days. This day however, as we were bundled against the ever-buffering wind and cold, with clouds sweeping by on and off, the green canvas shelter provided by the cook tent was most welcome.

When we arrived at camp late afternoon, next to a running fresh water creek formed by snowmelt that spouted out from the rock façade, we were at just over 13,000 feet in elevation, with still over 6,000 feet to go to reach the summit. The evening lighting offered surreal vistas both above and below as the rising thermal winds chased billowing clouds up the steep canyons from far below where the twinkling lights of Moshi town were at times visible. In the opposite direction and appearing insurmountable was the rock and ice face on top of which perched the summit of Mt. Kilimanjaro, somewhere way up in the sky. The setting sun lit the black rock cliffs, twinkling eerily with their melting glacial features. Our orange two-man tents provided a welcome respite from the damp cold, and I slipped off for the night, wondering where the trail might lead next.

I awoke early on day 4 of the climb at 6:40 a.m., realizing that if all went as planned that in about twenty-four hours our entire group, along with the Drake team and support staff, would be on top of Kili. I was anxious to get moving, even though my leg muscles were now aching, and my feet balked at being slipped inside my hiking boots.

The sun burned off the wispy moisture layer just as we started, having once again received clear instructions from our head guide about what the day would bring. After a downhill warm-up of a couple hundred yards the guides led us across the Barranco Wall, where we often had to keep at least one hand attached to the rock face in order to maintain balance. As I watched the first couple dozen hikers inch along the face, carefully picking hand and footholds, the actual trail become a bit more visible. What had appeared to be a treacherous rock face was actually quite passable, but did require constant communication among all of us. The leaders encouraged us while picking the very safest routes.

Those in the middle of the pack moved ahead stealthily, while the slower ones toward the back (me included) just continued to follow the leaders. Up, across, up, down, up, lean into the rock, up, use our quads, up, a couple small leaps, up and over. It took about an hour for each hiker to get over the Wall, meaning our entire team of hikers-turned-climbers made it safely to the semiflat section above in two hours.

A keen sense of accomplishment rose among the team as we realized this new barrier had been crossed, and the route wasn't too bad, all things considered. Everyone took a few moments to stand up tall on the massive flat boulders, gaze far, far down into the lush, green valley now framed by the cliffs we had just scaled. A powerful way to start the day!

From there it was more of a gentle rock scramble until around lunch time when our chosen trail turned decidedly uphill. At this point there was an option to continue on one of two trails, to head upwards toward the summit, or to divert and go downhill. If one continued on straight ahead toward the east, the trail would head over the next ridge, and then connect to another well-traveled path that went down the mountain.

Our lead guide offered this personal choice to each hiker, as the cooks prepared hot tea, chocolate, and coffee on this windswept rocky bluff. For me, there really was no choice, and I believed the same to be true for nearly everyone in our group, on our team. By turning left to go up the mountain a commitment was made, just as each had done at various points along the trail.

In reality, the personal commitments were made many months ago, and simply reinforced since then, monthly, weekly, and hourly over the past few days on Kilimanjaro. Funny thing about commitment though, the definition of which is clear: "An engagement or obligation that restricts freedom of action; a pledge or undertaking." We all know people for whom a commitment is not so much a vow or promise as it is a likely direction, suggestion, an anticipated result or goal. I say crap!

Once a commitment is made, it is an obligation to follow through.

Three of the Mexican students decided they could not make it further and took the trail that led them straight, then down. A simple physical aspect played out at this time. Football is a sport where sheer bulk can be an advantage, depending on the position played. Unfortunately, that trait does not relate well to hiking, and some of the young men who could not make it all the way were the linemen whose bodies were not designed to accomplish long hikes, which reward stamina over size.

Everyone else turned uphill, into the wind, on through the swirling cloud bank that enveloped each individual's body, but more importantly the minds and spirits that had just re-committed to success.

Two more arduous hours uphill brought us to camp, which was somehow squeezed in among piles of rocks and worn dirt trails. Bodily extremities were covered at all times except when needed to perform a delicate activity, like zipping up one's coat. The chill of the darkening late afternoon was pervasive, chasing all into their tents and causing more than a few to question what the final hike to the summit might be like.

As I was resting pre-dinner, thinking about what the night and the next morning would hold I heard a familiar, friendly voice, that of Frank Mella. I was fully clothed in my sleeping bag; head covered, so for a moment I thought the altitude was perhaps messing with my hearing. It was Frank! I quickly called out and climbed out of my bag and tent to hug my dear friend who had been the past four days on the opposite side of the mountain with the Drake entourage. I questioned how he got to our camp, to which he quipped, "Walked." He figured it had taken him about three hours to get from their pre-summit camp to ours, and he just felt compelled to come check on the Mexico group, say hello to them and to me, and wanted to wish us well on the impending summit climb. His presence instantly brought energy to my body, realizing the additional six-hour round trip he was making just to check on us, to ultimately "do his job" as my/our mountain outfitter. He had long ago earned my total respect for his professionalism and attention to detail, but this took it to a whole other level! He stayed just long enough for some hot tea we shared in the cook tent next to the roaring propane tanks which were warming the evening's dinner, then was gone off into the clouds, alone, back to the Drake climbers.

We committed to one another to meet on top in the early morning!

If I had any doubt about whether I would personally make it to the summit, and honestly I had never questioned this, that was entirely gone now. "See you at the Summit," he yelled back over his shoulder as he strutted off.

Before bed, a few more of the student athletes from my group met with the lead guide and head coach, deciding they were not going to make it and wanted to head down.

I was an ardent listener during that meeting, staged inside a weatherworn wooden building that just about fit the ten or so who attended. While I understood that a few of these healthy young men might be overmatched by the mountain, and the toll it had already taken on their bodies, I could not help but think that for most of them it was simply a mental defeat. After all, the guys in this meeting were nineteen to twenty-three years old, healthy and strong, trained to play a tough sport, to work hard and win. What caused some of them to give up, while their teammates, and coaches who were decades older and not nearly in peak physical condition, chose to continue? Was this a case of poor leadership, as it is always easy to follow someone "downhill," to take the path that is simply easier and less challenging? I believe it was really one young man, a peer who the others looked up to who sadly decided the summit goal was not worth the effort. Then, regrettably, the "followers" found it easy to do the same.

Some just want to succeed more than others! For them, the attainment of a goal was what motivated them. The metaphor of achieving a summit in life was not a metaphor here, but a reality. When this small group headed back down the trail, defeated I believed, toward the warmth and comfort the others of us would also find just one day later, I felt extremely sad for them. They would never in their lives, most likely, have the chance again to make it to the top of Mount Kilimanjaro, to stand there proudly.

I wondered how each of them would feel about this decision when they reflected upon it in a few days, months, or years. What would they tell their children about their particular Kili climb?

Bedtime came early that evening as we wanted to get as much rest as we could before our wake-up call at 10:00 p.m. to start the final ascent to the top. Frank and Amani had discussed the timing of the separate groups' departures, based upon hiking speed, distance and difficulty, in hopes of having as many as possible meet at Gilman's Point, which is where the various uphill trails intersect. It is on the southern edge of the carved-out caldera, some five hundred feet and about a half-hour walk from the ultimate summit. In addition, within our own hiking team there was a wide variety of speeds that had been obvious over the previous four days on Kili.

During most of days' hikes I would usually join a group towards the back, but not the last, which also included Coach Maya and Carmelo and a few other adult coaches. For the most part I found them to be conversant, engaging and full of *chispa de la vida* throughout the hike, and figured tonight would be more of the same.

The plan was for our subgroup of five adults to start at 11:00 p.m., about an hour before the entire rest of younger teammates. Following a delicious hot soup, bread, and veggie meal we strapped on our individual headlamps, snapped up our gators, grabbed the handy aluminum walking sticks, and fell in line behind our guide and the others. The night was moonless, but crystal clear and full of stars. Instantly I regained warmth throughout my body that can only be attained by walking steadily uphill, and this was definitely uphill. I had wondered aloud how we would find our way up the final 5,000 feet in elevation change in the dark, but found it very simple…just follow the guy in front.

There was not much conversation during the initial few hours, as basic breathing was tough enough. After about an hour on the trail I could spot a winding trail of dim headlights behind and below us, steadily moving our way, as it was clear the younger hikers were gaining on us, which was to be expected. I recalled the chase scene from *Butch Cassidy and the Sundance Kid*, when Robert Redford (Sundance) inquired about the posse following their trail, "Who are those guys?"

Frank was experienced enough to know how many guides we would need in order to maintain safety within the large horde of hikers, and ultimately we broke down into subgroups of about four to seven persons with each guide. I had my outer windbreaker mostly unzipped, my down vest half zipped, my gloves secured, wool hat on, and off, controlling the heat through my "chimney." For me it didn't seem overly difficult, but rather just one foot in front of the other. Step, walking stick pokes into the dirt/rock, quad flexes as the toes bend, push off, and repeat, repeat, repeat, repeat, repeat.

I did have my watch on but opted not to make the effort to view it very often. Instead I preferred to concentrate on thinking positive thoughts and realize that if I just kept moving, I would achieve my goal, as would all the others. Personally, the difficult part became the number of stops and resting periods that the others in my little gang were starting to take. Each time a small number of players would reach us, not only would we stop and step aside for them to pass by, but more often than not my allies would sit down, drink some water, rest, and eventually rise and begin again. This was wearing on me, as I much preferred just to keep moving, polé, polé! This halting process was starting to wear on me about the time it appeared there were no more lights behind us on the trail; they had all gone on ahead.

As I wondered how to handle this, wanting to assist my friends as well as accomplish personal goals, my mind drifted off the other seventy-five or so from Drake, who were likely having the same experience, just around the side of the mountain to the northeast of us.

I knew teamwork and motivation were essential to everyone who had taken on the challenge to climb Kilimanjaro, and knowing Coach Creighton; I was certain he had preached this all the way up, just as he did during the many months of preparation before the trip.

Coach's mantra could be seen in a Drake linebacker's blog accounting his final night's hike: "After about three hours of climbing in the pitch black I see another member of the group fall off. I hold back with him. I encourage him, and the conviction in his voice tells me that he is going to make it to the top. After about an hour of slow-paced walking, when no other groups were in sight, the porter and I convinced him to shed his pack and climb using my taller walking stick. The porter encourages me to go on; explaining that my teammate's conversing with me will only make it harder for him at this point. The porter has him covered. I give my ally, my school partner, my ever-closer friend the last of my water and start running up the mountain."

The climber he is referring to wasn't alone in his struggle to make it to the top. As the night wore on the trail became evermore steep, frustratingly slippery with gravel and with fewer rocks to use as handholds. Nobody could see the trail more than a few feet ahead, as it was quite vertical so that the headlamps would only illuminate a small area about waist-high when looking straight ahead. Plus it was getting colder as the night moved toward early pre-dawn hours, which again was to be expected, especially as we went up and up and up.

At one point while taking another of the far-too-frequent breaks due to my buddies needing to stop so often, I realized that I was getting exhausted and cold. If I continued to proceed at this pace the reality was that I might not make it to the top, and that was absolutely not an option! Option? Go down? Definitely not, but I was worried that the chill and fatigue would just overtake me while I lay down on the steep side-hill.

So I told my three close friends, and our guide, that I needed to move ahead without stopping. I told them that I was not leaving them, but rather simply blazing the trail for them! They understood, we wished one other luck and committed to meeting at the summit. Their commitment, however, did not sound nearly as serious as mine, as I knew they were having some very serious doubts about their personal stamina.

Gladly nobody I was with incurred any symptoms of edema, which would have necessitated the individual to go back down. That was my biggest fear, personally, as edema is a serious matter and once it starts to show itself the wise hiker has little choice but to turn around. Our primary limiting factor was oxygen, as breathing continued to grow more and more labored as the altitude increased and the hours on the mountain extended. This lack of oxygen led to leg muscle fatigue, and also to cold.

I pressed on alone, but not really, as I could still see a swerving line of headlamps ahead, and up…always up. We were all tired, weak and weary, trying not to trip, stumble and fall in our final ascent. It took everything we had to persevere.

I clearly remember what was going through my mind, drawing upon numerous and seriously challenging past life experiences, recalling them to reignite my own mental toughness.

I thought back to high school football 3-a-day practices in the mid-sixties in the stifling heat and humidity at Camp Notre Dame in Erie, when we were not allowed to drink water until after practice.

My mind then floated back to my Machu Picchu Inca Trail hike in 1977 with two acquaintances from the British Antarctic Survey, coercing my quads to carry me up the steep passes the native Inca had run up and over centuries ago.

My memory clearly recalled how in 1979, I had led our small groups of clients up the precipitous slopes of Volcán Acatenango in Guatemala, loaded down with sixty-four pounds of fresh water as well as my own personal belongings, just so we could witness the magnificent explosions of nearby Volcán Fuego at sunset.

Hawaii came into view, The Big Island, as Janet and I and a few client friends ambled up the mild slope of Mauna Loa, thinking that the 13,679-foot volcanic top was something very special, which it was. I then instantly moved my vision from the mountain to peacefully sailing the Kona Coast with the same friends a few days later, drifting with the trade winds.

Then, I allowed myself to reminisce about some of most special and fulfilling moments of my life, thinking back to walking through the expansive Gila Wilderness of New Mexico with my wife and young children, offering them an appreciation of nature and all its wonders.

And as if it had just occurred in recent months I had a vision of my wedding day, patiently awaiting my incredible wife, Janet, to arrive in all her splendor and beauty, though tardy as always, and stroll down the aisle towards me with her hair perfectly braided with sweet flowers.

Visions of each of my children abruptly came to the front of my thoughts, each of them gleefully carrying handfuls of bluebonnets picked from our Texas pastures, their smiles beaming as our fluffy grey cats followed along.

Each of these visions and thoughts helped to pass the time, which was all I needed to succeed, just more time and sustained energy.

Music kept jumping in and out of my altitude-dulled brain, some topical, other just random, but each song from a poignant portion of my own personal history. James Brown topped the charts with "I Feel

Good," which had become my personal "prepractice stretching hype song" on all our Global Football tours.

Then a bit of "Willin'" by Willie Nelson. "And I been from Tucson to Tucumcari..."

"Desperado" by the Eagles, as I recalled most all the words. "Why don't you come to your senses, you been out ridin' fences for so long now!"

Suddenly, a very odd song I had not thought of in years would slip into my consciousness: "I'm Henry the Eighth. I am, Henry the Eighth I am I am, I got married to the widow next door...." by Herman's Hemits. Where did that come from?

A little Temptations always smooths things out. "I got sunshine on a cloudy day, and when it's cold outside, I got the month of May."

Then there was my old downhill ski beat by Urszula Dudziak, with the repetitive instrumental chorus, which so often carried me over the bumps of Steamboat decades ago.

Of course, the victory refrain by Queen, "No time for losers cause we are the champions of the world."

All these, and more, flowed in and out of my thoughts as I continued gasping for air, stepping ever upward. Polé, polé! There were moments, brief thoughts, creeping into my weary brain, where I questioned my stamina and ability to finish this climb. But those only lasted a few seconds before returning to the task at hand, which was simply to reach the summit; to complete the journey, to achieve the goal I had set for myself, along with all these other young men who had set the same goal.

Then there was something different in the sky. Out of nowhere appeared a dim orange light up ahead, over the top of a somewhat visible charcoal dark ridge; to the east...the sun was beginning to rise over far off Kenya!

If morning was coming, then so was Gilman's Point, and the summit of Africa's tallest mountain! With the ever-brightening light came ever-renewed energy. My body was warming and rejuvenating as my stride quickened though the severity of the pitch never diminished, and even appeared more vertical. That didn't matter now, however, as the goal was in sight, and nothing was going to stop our entire team of hikers from making it to the top.

The head guides for the two groups had previously coordinated their departure times from the two different camps so that we could meet one another. They had radio contact most of the time and were constantly in touch when geography allowed, filling each other in on their locations. As it turned out, they timed it nearly perfectly. No rookies were leading this trip!

As my vision slipped over the cinder crest and looked ahead to the gravel bowl below, and onto the very near actual summit just around this caldera, I also gazed upon the heavily jacketed silhouette of Coach Chris Creighton as he ambled toward me along the ridge from the east. He had a huge sparkling smile shining through his weathered cheeks, further darkened by his five-day growth of beard. I eased a few steps in his direction; we instantly locked eyes, embracing as only two brothers of kindred spirit could do, as two sons of God were moved to do, giving thanks for our many gifts and for the safety and success of everyone with us.

Chris Creighton is simply an amazingly wonderful man, whose idea this was. I felt so blessed and proud to be able to share this moment, this gift with him, and with his Drake team, along with the Mexican team which had also performed so admirably.

After the two teams met at Gilman's Point, arriving in scatterings of three to eight persons each over about a half-hour's time, we gathered and completed the last hour of our climb together, as one team, reaching the summit of Mount Kilimanjaro. While not steep, this final stretch still took all of our remaining effort due to the lack of oxygen at this altitude and the fact that we had hiked through the night for eight hours.

Just as we reached Uhuru Peak, the highest point of Kili, the sun rose just enough to light up the entire side of the mountain.

At 19,341 feet, with incredible exhilaration, we felt like kings on top of the world! There were hugs, kisses, sweat and tears.

Not only did we have the personal satisfaction of making it to the highest point in Africa, but our teams had also made history. Of the 135 people who began this hike together, 90 percent reached the top!

Never before, that anyone could find, had 120 hikers stood on the top of Mount Kilimanjaro at one time!

To top it off, we brought with us what we believe to be the youngest climber to ever summit, Sandy and Jeff Clubb's nine year old daughter Skyler who made the entire trip on her own two feet along with her older year old brother Tristan.

Photographs were taken by various groups of teammates, friends, families, team positions, guides with hikers, coaches with players, Mexicans and Americans and Tanzanians, all together, having committed and succeeded.

As soon as I reached the summit I proudly pulled from the top of my backpack three prized items that, while extremely light in weight, did bear down on me throughout the five days' hike. They manifested upon me the burden of knowing I could not fail to bring the national colors of Tanzania, Mexico, and the United States of America to the top of Kilimanjaro. These three symbols stood as the props for everyone's photos, proudly flapping in the bitter, steady wind rising up from the south face and hurling itself over the rocky summit.

All together we represented three nations standing in unity on top of Africa!

View from the Summit-Really!

Seventeen months prior two men had met. They were already friends, having shared prior experiences. They were both dreamers, and were both doers, who believed in one another, and in the power of God.

One of these men had a dream he shared with the other, which he had already shared with a woman who was his boss, who was also a dreamer, and a doer, with similar faith.

The two men searched the world for seven months until they found a willing third partner, a Mexican university administrator with immense vision. He also was dreamer, and a doer.

These three men and one lady, living in Iowa, Texas, and Monterrey, Mexico, decided they would take two football teams from two bordering nations halfway around the world to play the first American football game ever played on the African continent, one of the seven on earth.

They dreamed of having a major impact, in many ways, on a third country, Tanzania.

In this country, they would spend seventeen days, with each of the twenty-four-hour periods filled with joy, excitement, wonder, and prayers of thanks.

While in Tanzania they spent three days playing football, two playing with and interacting with youngsters on a football field; three days doing community service work in schools, hospitals, and orphanages; one to six days on jungle safaris; six days heading up and down Mount Kilimanjaro, and countless hours smiling, laughing, exploring, and experiencing.

Two collegiate football teams from neighboring, albeit all too often politically embattled nations, led by passionate individuals dreamed of making history, and making a difference, in a third country halfway around the world. They committed, shared, grew, enjoyed, and succeeded.

13

Climbing Realities—Life Lessons—Mil Gracias

You only get one chance at life to leave your mark upon it. And when a pony he comes riding by, you better set your sweet ass on it.
 —Zac Brown Band, as written in my Tanzania Diary

Patrick at University of Notre Dame, 1971

As both teams met up once more at the Episcopal Church Youth Hostel in Moshi to shower, change, repack, and enjoy one last meal together, excitement as well as a sort of melancholy feeling filled the air. The tour had turned out to be everything I could have dreamed and more, but the last hours of our time in Tanzania together were upon us, and nobody wanted to see it end. This was our final meal all together, and thus a perfect time for our awards banquet before the Mexicans had to depart for the airport and their long journey back home.

Fortunately, the Drake team had one more night in Arusha to recuperate before their flight home the following evening. The extra day gave them some down time to do the more tourist-style activities in the area. Most of the team ended up making a stop at the expansive Cultural Heritage Center, which holds the largest and most varied collection of art, photographs, antiques and jewelry from East Africa. We also spent much of the last day shopping for gifts and souvenirs for friends and family back home.

A year later I thought it would make sense to look back and see exactly what resulted out of this event? I mean, we all participated; it made us feel good…in fact it, made us feel great! But what kind of tangible results could we point to afterward?

First let's start with the folks in Tanzania.

Tanzania

This event had a massive economic impact on the local Tanzanians.

The Kili Bowl stimulated the economy tremendously, providing cash flow for regional, national and local businesses alike, including government workers and all of the institutions and associations we worked with to make this event possible. It also provided temporary work for over a thousand people, including those who helped us up the mountain, guided us through the parks, assisted in setting up the stadium and tended to our every need in the hotels.

Socially, this event also had considerable influence on the people of Tanzania. As Frank Mella put it, "Everyone in Tanzania who was involved or participated in this event in one way or another, has learned something about Mexican and American traditions. The game was totally unknown to many Tanzanians and, much more so than any other sports we have learned that the American football game has something to do with solidarity. Through this event, we were able to bring together many local schools' pupils and the visiting students to talk, to learn, to play and to share the experience with Americans and Mexicans; even now there are so many all over Arusha wearing the shirts with the Kili Bowl logo and Drake shirts. And we can still see the balls around town that were given to over 1,000 youngsters!"

The more tangible social results though can be seen through our far-reaching community service efforts. There is now a school that has a cement volleyball court which will give pleasure to young children for years to come, enjoyment they may not necessarily be able to have in other aspects of their lives. An orphanage now has six brand new bedrooms that can house four bunk beds each, creating space for forty-eight children in desperate need of a roof over their heads. There is a school, freshly sanded and painted, where children can go to learn and hopefully be given more opportunities than those before them were provided. There is a chicken coop to supply chickens a safe place to lay eggs, an essential and sustainable part of a healthy diet for young orphaned Tanzanians. Trees were planted; school foundations were built and through this, individual lives were changed forever. The work didn't stop when we left; we were merely the catalysts for change. These service efforts were able to provide the YES alumni students with a jump-start on changing their communities for the better.

While visiting Tanzania I learned of the dire need for fresh water wells in the rural areas of the country, where entire villages will spend the majority of their waking hours simply in search of fresh water. Generally the gathering is done by the mothers and children, keeping them from other tasks like mothering, attending school, etc.

Shortly after returning from the Kili Bowl event and realizing what an impact it had on me personally, I felt compelled to do more for the Tanzanian people. Working through the Tanzania Water Project which is headed up by Arizonan Dean Riesen and coordinated in country by Lazaro

Nyalandu, I decided to donate funds to construct a well and all the above ground items needed for a village in the Singida Region. It is the least I could do, and something I plan to do more of through using profits from this book.

Drake University

At the team banquet the night before Drake left for the United States, one of the Drake team members, Cam Good showed Coach Creighton a photo. The photo was that of a teammate, Pat Cashmore, a soon-to-be-fifth-year senior. Pat was touching the sign at the top of Mt. Kilimanjaro. He told Coach that while doing so, his group had said out loud that they had a vision of kissing the Pioneer Football League (PFL) trophy. The next day Drake headed back to Iowa where in the fall they went on to become the Pioneer Football League Conference co-champions, having only two losses in their regular season. Pat Cashmore was the first one handed the trophy, which he proceeded to kiss and hold up for all to see. His vision, his dream, had come true.

Winning that season certainly wasn't easy, but a lot of what was accomplished in Africa helped make it a reality. At summer training camp before the season began Coach Creighton introduced his players to the Six Climbing Realities: "This camp is an opportunity for our new family members to learn about the importance of our Six Climbing Realities—realities that we have learned through years of playing football and from actually climbing the largest free standing mountain in the world. These last four years have all been a part of the process and the journey. We are now ready to get to the top. TUPANDE KILELENI means *Let's Climb to the Summit, Together.* This is what we are doing in 2011—it is our time to Climb to the Summit together."

Coach Creighton used Tupande Kileleni as the theme for the season. He drew up a scene of the mountain with six stops along the way which were the six climbing realities:

1. Climbing Takes Preparation
2. Climbing Takes Sacrifice

3. Climbing Takes Teamwork
4. Climbing Takes Going One Step at a Time
5. Climbing Takes a Competitive Spirit
6. Climbing Takes Overcoming Adversity

He had these displayed via a slideshow, which he presented every Monday in the team meeting. He believed that every week in the regular season was a microcosm of the entire journey and it was important to constantly be reminded to go through each of the six climbing realities for every facet of the climb. Coach also put together a "Champions Manual" at the beginning of the season to help players reflect upon what they wanted to achieve through what they had learned in Tanzania. In it, he included passages that each of his players had written about the six climbing realities. These passages provided a deep insight as to just how much the Kili Bowl affected their outlook on football and life in general.

Here are a few examples:

1. *Climbing Takes Preparation*—From Tyler Castro #12—Quarterback

> The old cliché of "confidence through preparation" is a saying that holds true on both the overwhelming base of the mountain and the battlefield of our stadium. The mountain was something that no one could really predict or anticipate, but by taking the necessary preparations we were able to attack and overcome each obstacle. We rested our bodies, learned from the advice of others, and didn't underestimate the challenge, which proved to carry us up 19,000 feet. When it comes to the game of football, we must be ready to approach each game with the same mindset and willingness to prepare ourselves. We have physically trained and conditioned our bodies and always have to be ready mentally to study and learn about our opponents. It is through this preparation that we will be able to charge onto the field with a fire in our hearts and a swagger in our

step that can ultimately take us to the summit of the Pioneer Football League.

2. *Climbing Takes Sacrifice-* From Alec Recker #23—Wide Receiver

    Vince Lombardi once said a great quote describing sacrifice: 'Success is like anything worthwhile. It has a price. You have to pay the price to win, and you have to pay the price to get to the point where success is possible. Most important, you must pay the price to stay there.' This quote truly hits sacrifice on the head; nothing is going to be easy this fall, and nothing was easy on the climb. If we're not willing to sacrifice day in and day out we will lose, everyone has to sacrifice with one thing in mind. The PFL Championship.

3. *Climbing Takes Teamwork*—From Tyler Mosier— Defensive Back (Took the position of Student Assistant Coach due to injury)

    To be the best that we can be and win our conference this year, it is going to take teamwork. While over in Africa we had different groups all the time, we had groups for what buses we were going to be on for the first couple days, groups for the kids camp, groups for the community service projects, and then finally groups for the hike. Why were these groups so special? It's because it made us have to come together and talk about who works best with each other, how each person works, and the strengths and weaknesses of each person. A good example I have for this is the group that went to the STEMM orphanage with me. We had to go paint blackboards for a school, paint the entrance gate, make concrete and build a chicken fence. Here our group divided up into what people could do, and since I couldn't lift much heavy stuff because of my hip, we decided it would be smart for me to paint and work on putting the chicken fence up, while others in our group were able to do concrete and hated to paint. To win the PFL this season we are going to have to look at everyone's strengths and weaknesses and be able to work together as an offense, defense and special teams.

4. *Climbing Takes Going One Step at a Time*—From Nick Gral #41—Defensive Line Coach

   The thing to remember at the start of the season is "Pole Pole." Although we may have what seems like a million things going on, taking each individual thing as it comes will allow us as a team to keep our heads level and plan for success.

   Pole Pole. One step at a time…

5. *Climbing Takes Competitive Spirit-* From Cam Goode #18—Linebacker

   Not only did I want to summit that mountain, I wanted to be the first. Our group was the first to leave and kept our focus throughout the entire climb. 7 hours later, my group was now only 100 yards away from being the first group from Drake to make it up to the mountain. We came; we saw, and we conquered. There was no person or thing in sight, just us and the mountaintop. As we reached the Uhuru Peak sign, something happened. I had a vision of us winning the PFL championship. As I saw Pat Cashmore kissing the sign, I also saw Pat Cashmore kissing the trophy cup. As our group celebrated with hugs and tears, I saw the same group celebrating in Drake Stadium. You can call me crazy, but it is something that I saw. Let's overcome adversity. Let's have a competitive spirit in every game we play. Let's get that championship!

6. *Climbing Takes Overcoming Adversity*—From Pat Cashmore #30—Running Back

(He had never finished a season, suffering from multiple knee injuries…until this one.) Viewing games from the sidelines has forced me to find other ways to support my teammates and has made my time on the field that much sweeter. Obstacles such as injuries and coaching changes have taught me that nothing is certain, and it's important not to get comfortable. Let's not be content with being middle of the pack of the PFL; let's win the championship. Entering my fifth year, I know that there is no next year. However, there is never a guarantee for a next year, so let this year be the best year of your career, and let's climb the mountain to the championship.

CONADEIP

For many of the Mexican players who were able to make it to the Kili Bowl, Dr. Enrique Ramos described this trip as "their most significant life experience." He explained that in many ways, through learning, understanding and experiencing the very different Tanzanian culture, they came to have a much deeper appreciation for their own Mexican culture. As with many aspects of life, this came to be especially true for those student athletes who were not as socially privileged as others. They were the ones who worked hard to raise the money to make the trip possible. Enrique went on to explain that it was mostly those students, the ones who weren't merely given everything in life, who made it to the top of Mt. Kilimanjaro. They were the ones who showed the heart and the desire to achieve great things. They had worked so hard to get to that point, and they weren't going to give up, no matter how difficult the climb.

Since the CONADEIP team was an all-star squad from a number of different universities, which compete against one another during the season, it was harder to measure their success as a unified football team. However, I was able to see tangible results at the annual Tazón de Estrellas event I help produce, the event through which I first met

Enrique. The game brings top NCAA Division III players from across the United States to Mexico to play against a Mexican All-Stars team. Of the sixty players on that all-star team, about thirty of them, most of whom were starters, were the guys who had gone to Tanzania. Prior to this December 2011 event the Americans had won eleven games while the Mexicans had won only two, with many of their losses being pretty good whippings by the USA team. This year, though, was different. This time, Team Stars and Stripes was soundly defeated, a huge victory by the CONADEIP All-Stars.

The CONADEIP head coach mentioned to me right after the game that a great deal of the teamwork and camaraderie seen this year had been developed through the work they had done in Tanzania.

Drake & CONADEIP

As previously mentioned, part of Enrique's job is to find universities around the world with whom they would like to share, learn and create a relationship. Enrique and Sandy, through their work on the Kili Bowl, developed both a personal friendship and a professional relationship, which has greatly helped to provide benefits to both Universities. Even before the Tanzania adventure Enrique enlisted Sandy's help, having her travel to Mexico to speak via CONADEIP's "Virtual University to the multiple universities" that make up the CONADEIP system. Her focus was on the students who participated in intercollegiate athletics, not only to develop them as athletes but as whole human beings. Enrique wanted her to share the mission statement of Drake University—developing Tec Monterrey's culture and values as well as their goals by integrating athletics into their campus. This was a primary reason she supported the decision for Drake to play a football game in Africa.

Not only did Sandy travel to Mexico to give this talk, she brought with her a handful of staff members from various departments at Drake, who are now connected with Tec Monterrey. Now, not only from an athletic perspective, but also from an academic one, the two schools are able to work with and learn from one another in hopes of creating better opportunities for their students. Currently, the two schools are involved with each other in many areas, highlighted by faculty exchange programs and clinics. This relationship is continuing to evolve, and it all started with the Kili Bowl.

Global Football and Myself

In the short run, from a business sense, the event honestly made no sense! I was lucky if I broke even financially on the event. But that wasn't what it ended up being about for me. Has it been good for my business since then? I think it has provided me with a whole other level of respect in the American football world as well as in the travel world. It is and always will be something I can hang my hat on until the day I die. I can proudly say I produced the first ever American Football game on the continent of Africa. This would be huge in any business. I can remember Dr. Christian Bernard, the South African doctor who did the first heart transplant. That was over forty years ago and a complete stranger and yet I still remember his name because he was the first. I can remember the night Wilt Chamberlain scored one hundred points, listening to it on my radio in the third floor dormitory of my home with my two brothers. Nobody has done it since which makes it that much more amazing. That first time for anything is so special, and I was totally committed to being the first in this case and so thankful to have done it.

I think in every business there are teams that can put things together, there are leaders, and there are groups who are just waiting to be led, wanting to be presented a dream to capture. So how does the Kili Bowl apply to other people?

Everyone out there who manages anything has some talented staff behind them. Energetic and eager with bright minds, they want to accomplish, to succeed. All it takes is motivation, and leadership. The people are there; it is just about molding them into a team and instilling a dream they can work together to develop.

I hope what my story does is inspire people to dream even bigger and to share their dreams like Coach Creighton did with me. If he had kept his dream to himself it would never have come true. There was a great cross-pollination enabling us to accomplish this event. Within this event, we had people from around the world and across the United States who fed off of one another with their thoughts and ideas to make it what it was. And all of this began with one person, with one dreamer.

After all is said and done I believe one of the key things is to give thanks to everyone. We all get remiss sometimes when we accomplish great things. We stand around and take the high fives; we get our pictures taken and then it is over, and we move on to the next life task. But giving thanks after the fact is critical. I did so a month after the event was over when I was moved to draft an email and send it out to everybody that was part of the whole event. In it, I thanked everyone for their help and congratulated them on their success. One year after the event I sent out yet another e-mail, remembering, giving thanks, and reminding them of their great achievements. Sometimes we get so caught up in everyday life, and we move onto the next goal, the next project, the next thing to achieve without remembering the great things we have done in the past with the help of many. I hope I remember this event each year, and I will continue give thanks to everyone who helped make it a success. We may lose track of each other as our lives move in different directions, but hopefully we keep track of the lives we have changed and the good we have accomplished along the way.

This event has and continues to impact the lives of countless individuals. Not only did it impact the young men on the football teams and their families, but also the coaches and their families who came along. This event changed the lives of countless Tanzanian men, women and children. The cultural exchange alone that went on between our three great nations was amazing and an experience you can't get on just any vacation.

For my daughter Xela, it enabled her to stay in Tanzania for another six weeks, working with the Arusha Lutheran Medical Center as a volunteer. She was able to travel often by bush plane along with nurses to distant villages serving the people there. From that experience, she has now moved onto graduate school in Ireland, working towards being a physical therapist where she will assist impaired children and adults for her working life.

If nothing else were to come out of this, the Global Kilimanjaro Bowl created a better understanding and appreciation among peoples from vastly different backgrounds who came together for a common cause. That, to me, is a successful business operation.

View to the Summit

In August 2013 I was on the grass field for pre-game warm-ups in Monterrey, Mexico as the Borregos of Tec de Monterrey were about to take on their arch-rival, the Tigres of UANL in front of fifty thousand animated fans. The buzz was palpable; tough young men were getting ready, getting pumped to play a rugged game, focusing on their impending matchup.

As I was gazing about and snapping photos a powerful, sweaty hand grabs me on the shoulder, "Coach Patrick, me recuerdes? Yo juge en Tanzania con usted, el Kili Bowl! Subi Kilimanjaro, apoye los huerfanos alla, encontre leones. Lo cambio mi vida totalmente. Mil gracias."

(Coach Patrick, remember me? I played in Tanzania with you in the Kili Bowl! I climbed Kilimanjaro, helped the orphans there, and encountered lions. It changed my life totally. A thousand thank you's.)

TUPANDE KILELENI:
LET'S CLIMB TO THE SUMMIT TOGETHER

CREATE YOUR TEAM;
DEVELOP THEIR DREAM